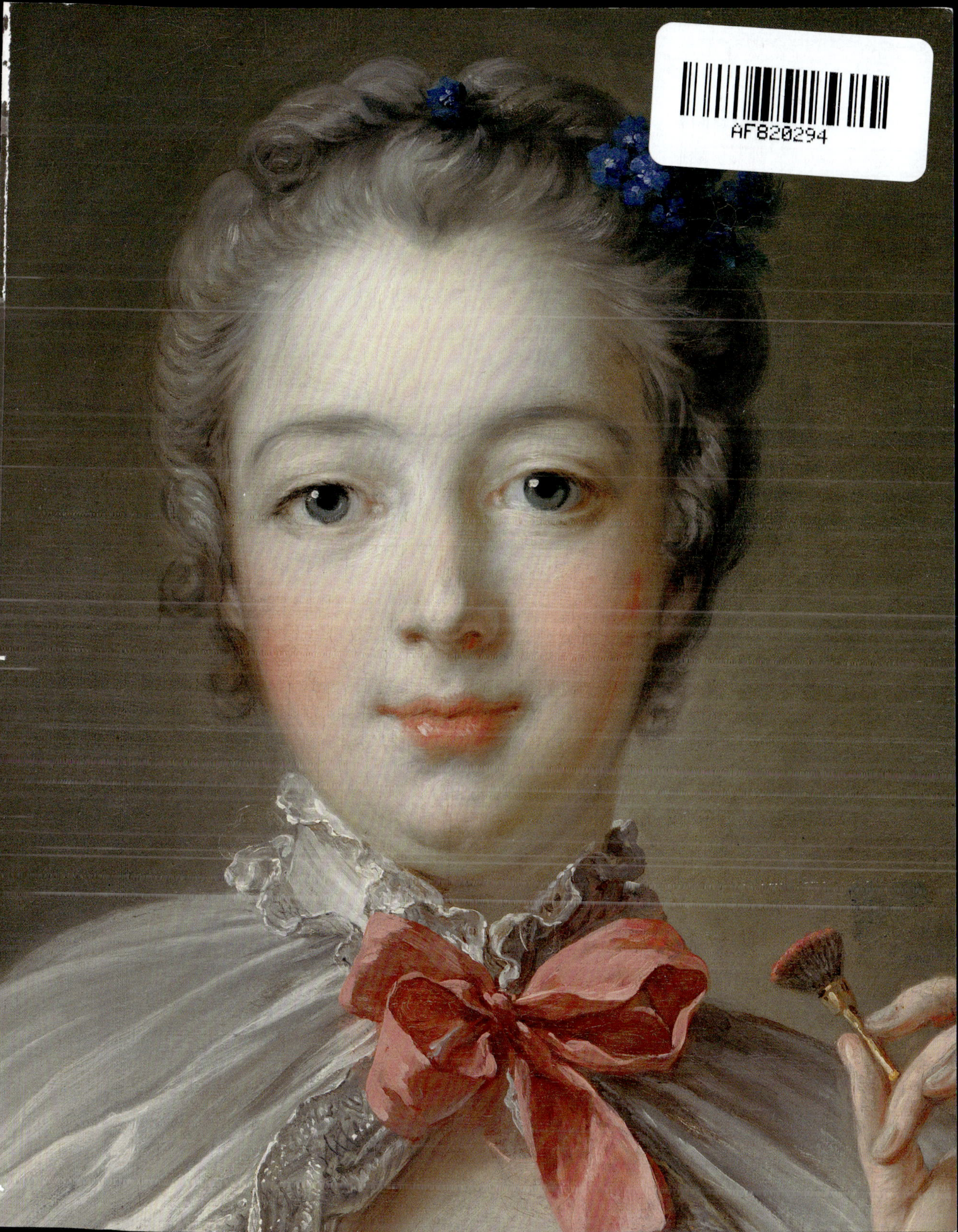

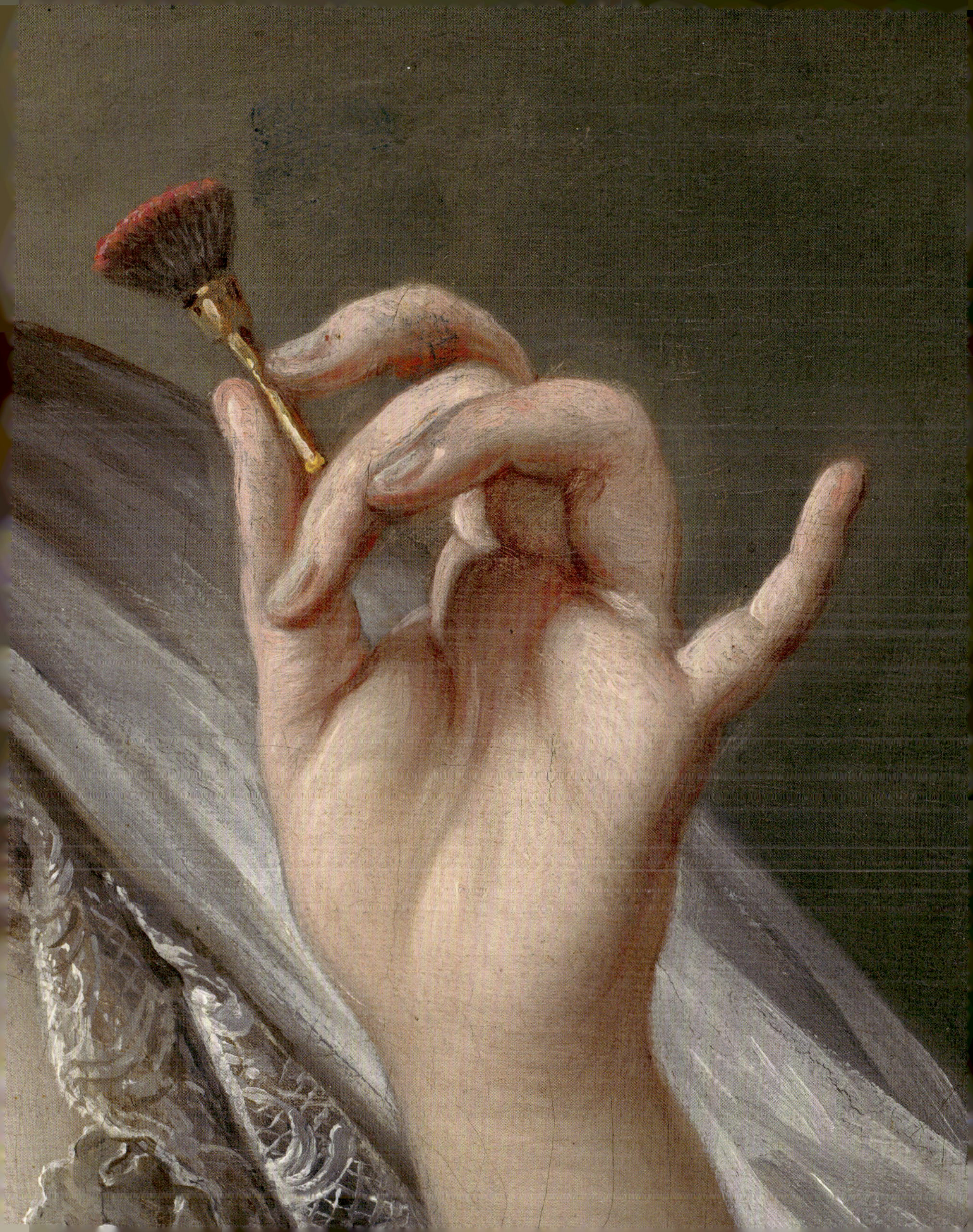

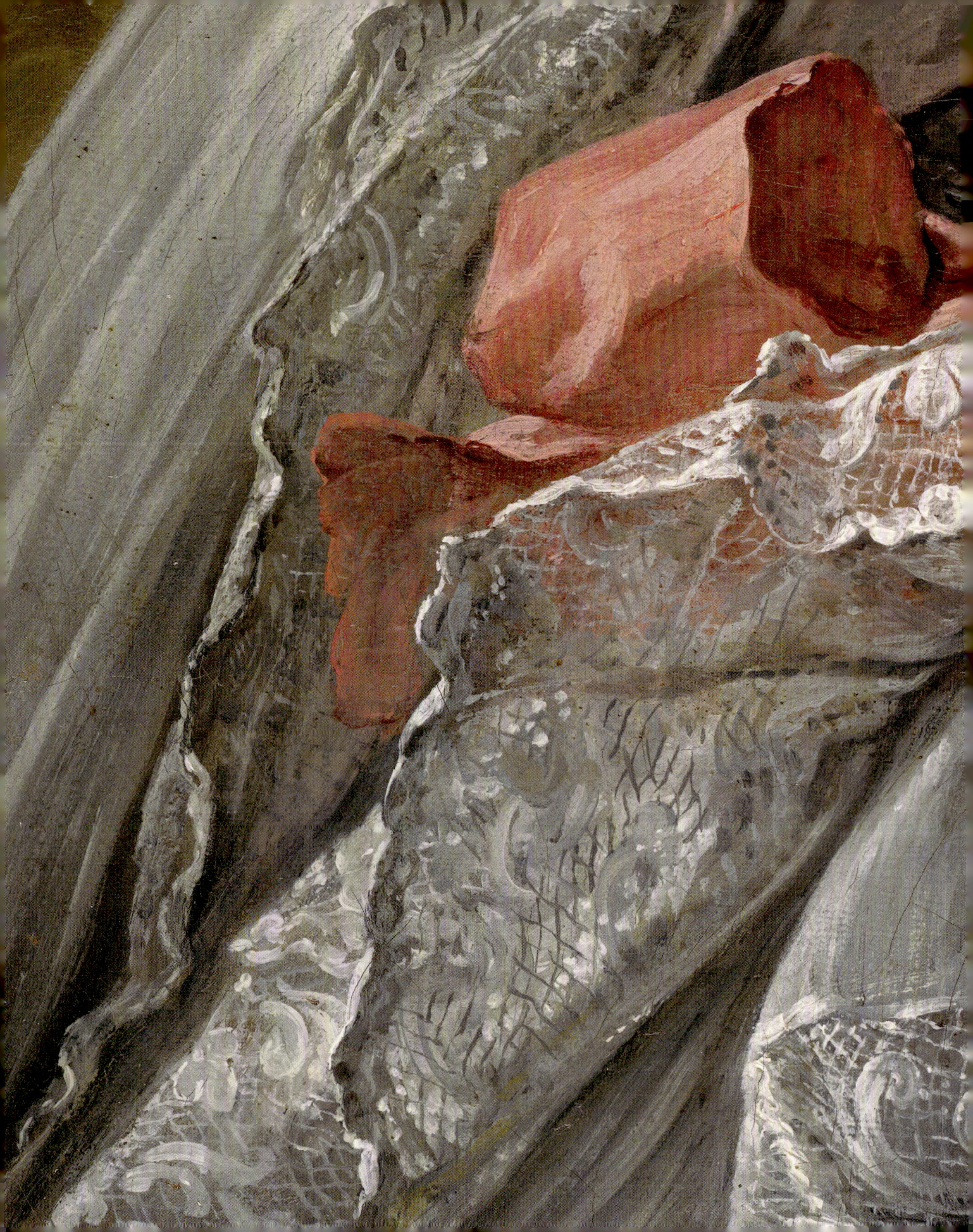

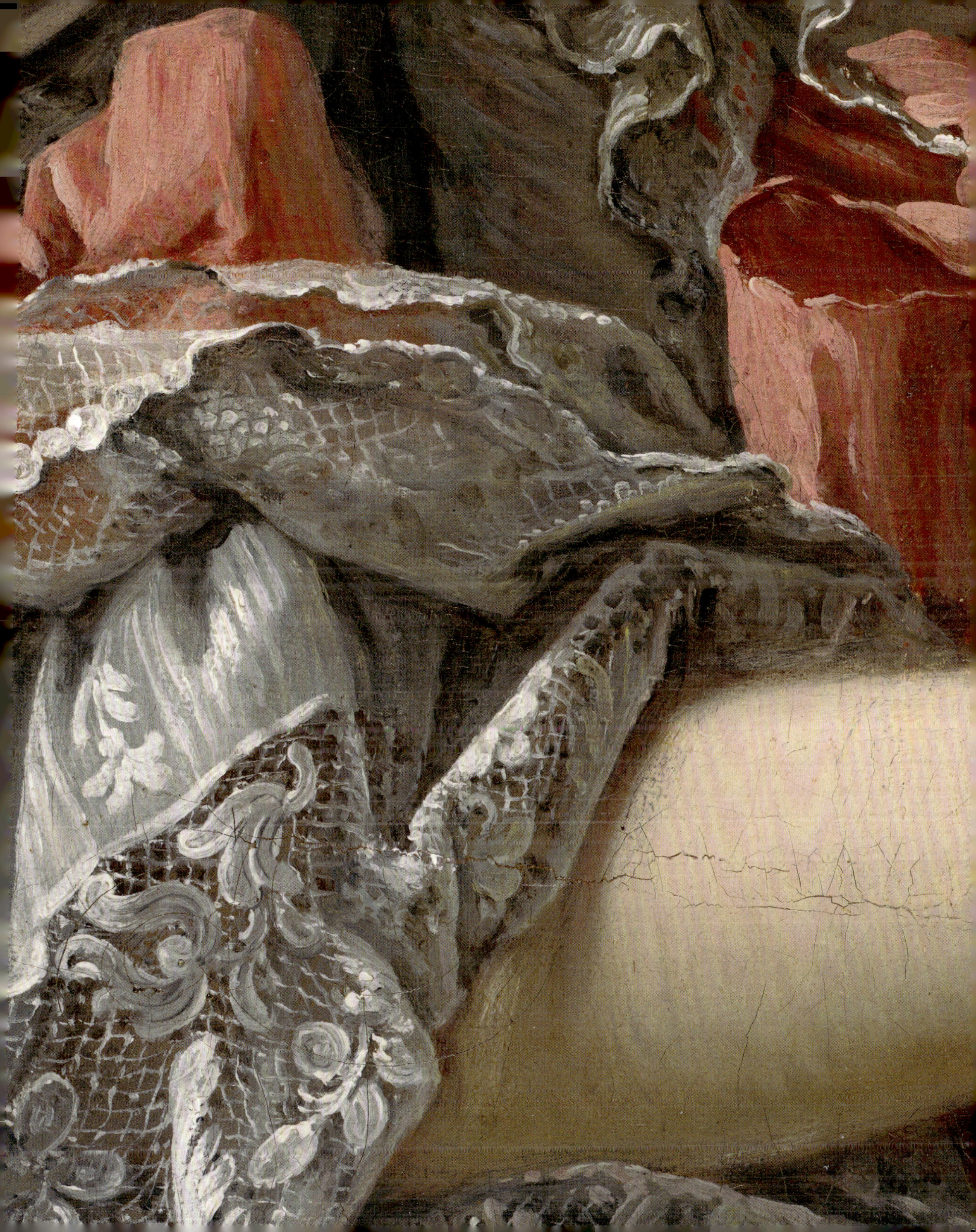

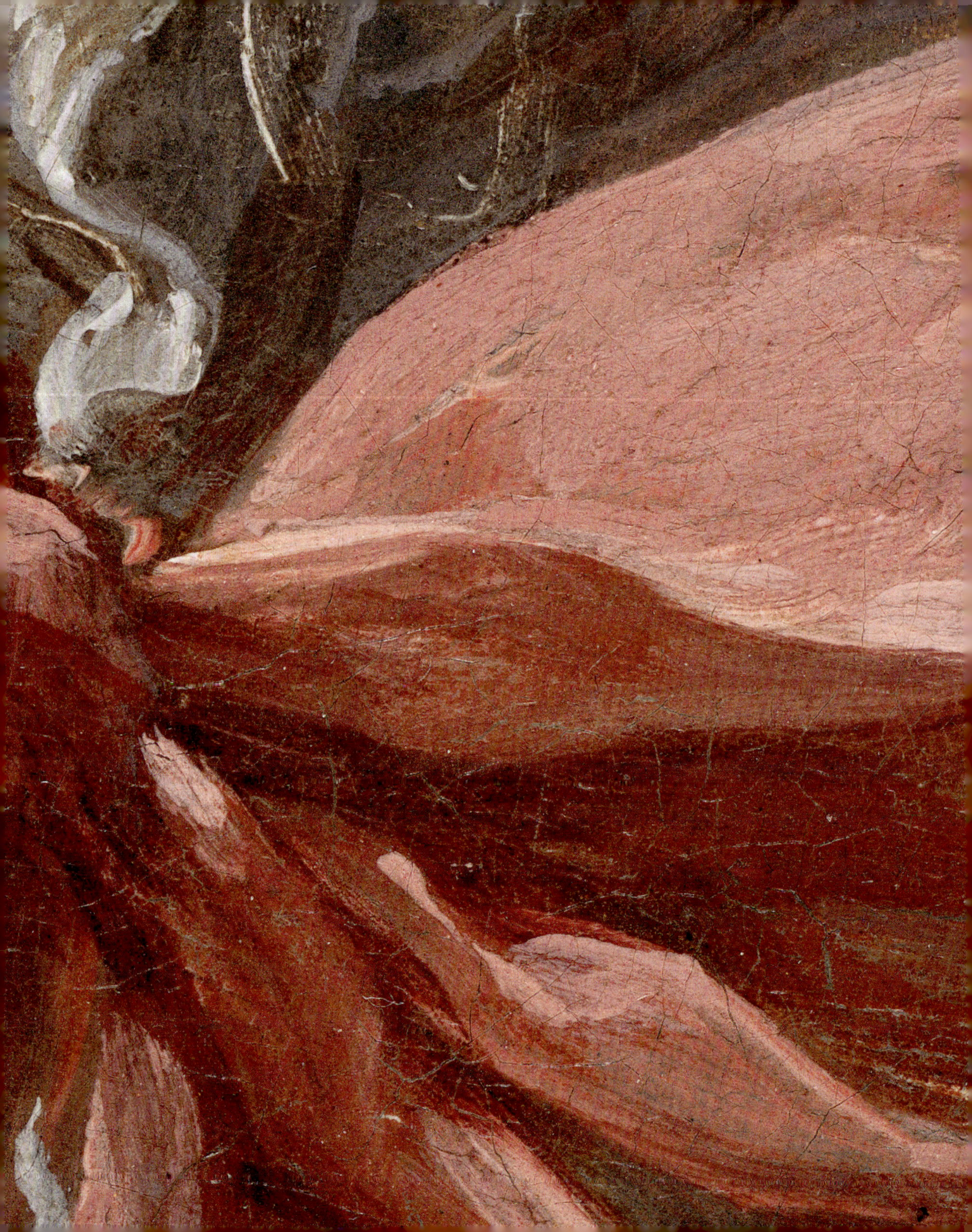

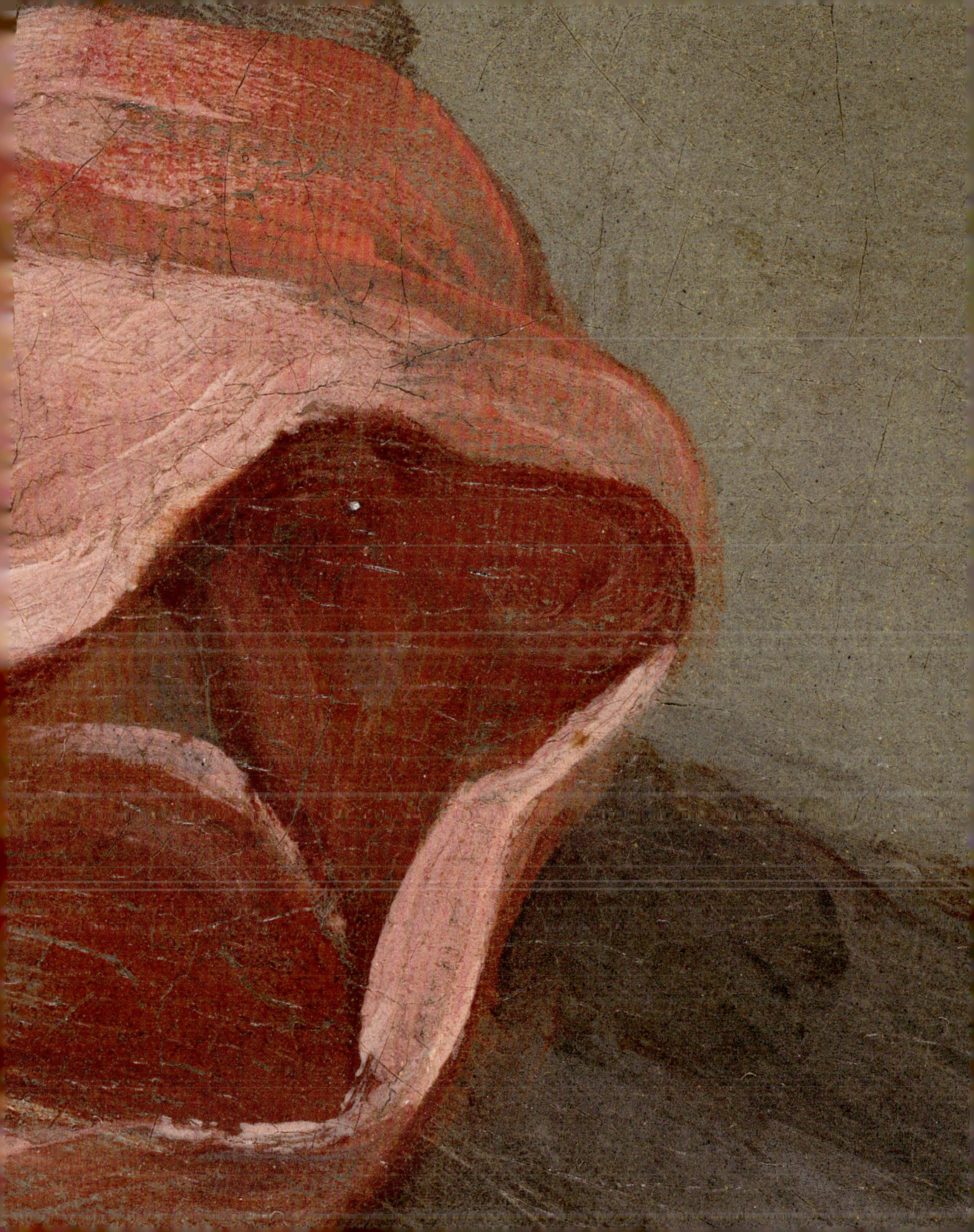

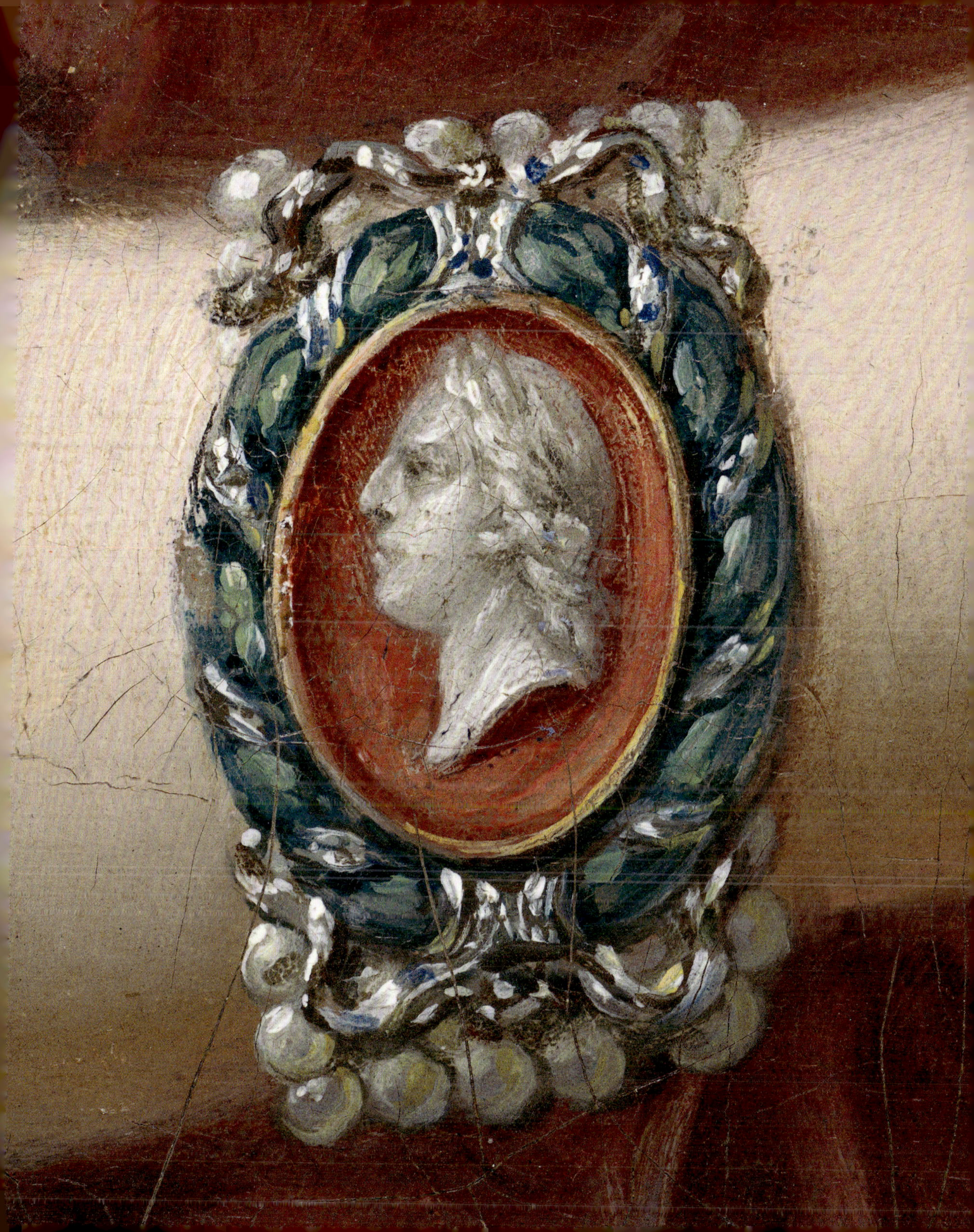

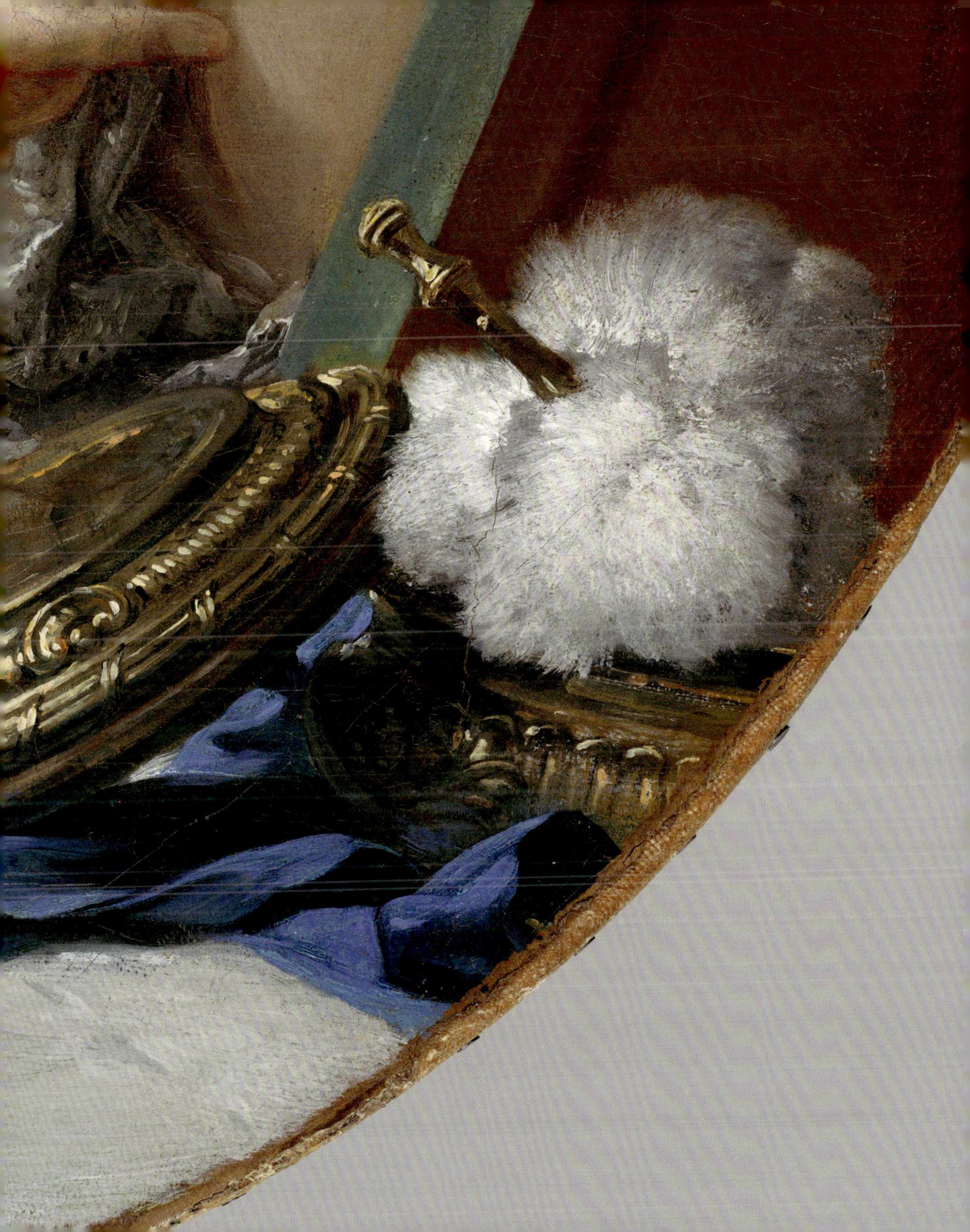

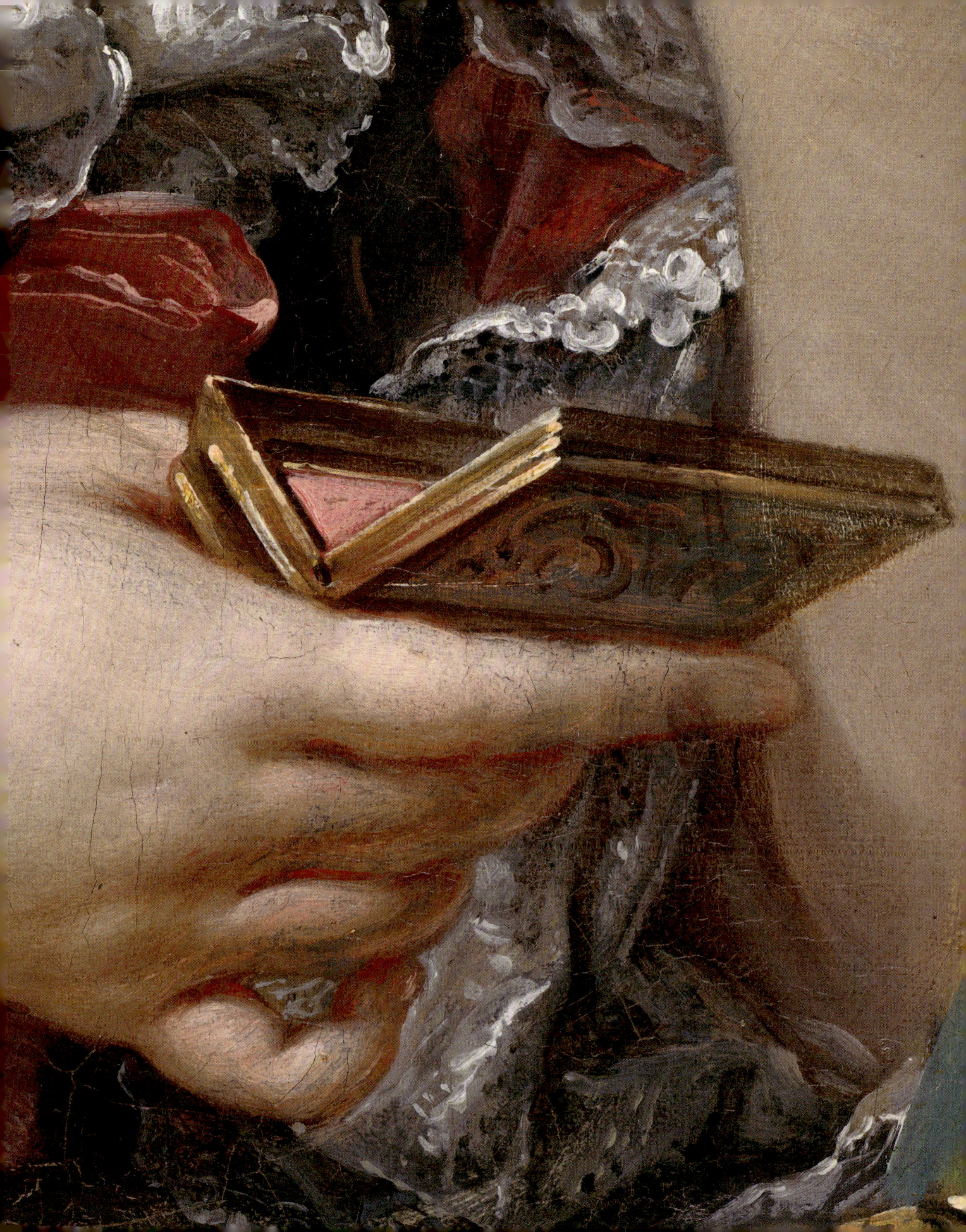

Pages 1–16:
François Boucher, *Pompadour at Her Toilette*, 1750, with later additions. Oil on canvas, 81.2 × 64.9 cm. Harvard Art Museums/Fogg Museum, Bequest of Charles E. Dunlap, 1966.47.

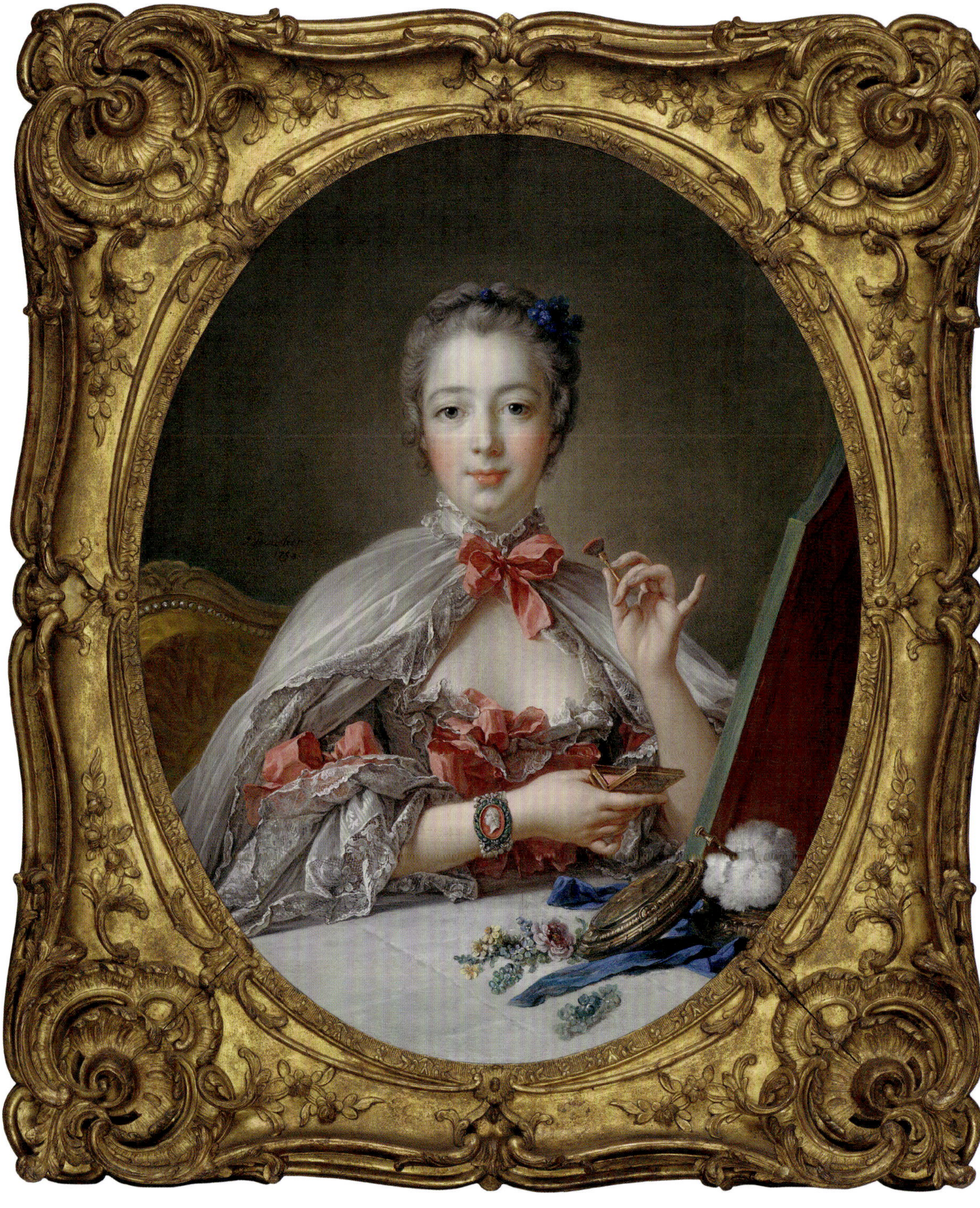

Madame de Pompadour

Painted Pink

Edited by

A. CASSANDRA ALBINSON

With contributions by

A. CASSANDRA ALBINSON
MARK LEDBURY
GABRIELLA SZALAY
OLIVER WUNSCH

Harvard Art Museums
Cambridge, Mass.

Distributed by Yale University Press
New Haven and London

Preface

FRANÇOIS BOUCHER DID NOT INVENT PINK, but he is perhaps the artist most associated with the color. In the nineteenth century, the Goncourt brothers—French authors and aesthetes—enthused that his pink was "tender and pale like a rain-soaked rose [*rose noyée*]."[1] Yet Boucher has also been criticized for overuse of this "feminine" color.[2] In paintings that predate his career, pink often appears in the clothing of the Virgin as she holds the baby Jesus (Fig. 1), suggesting a connection with maternal devotion. In Boucher's mythological works, it is common to see the powerful Venus, goddess of love, lying beneath yards of coral silk held aloft by dimpled putti. Similarly, in works such as his colored chalk drawing of a reclining nude, a naked woman is often propped against pink fabric (Fig. 2). This dual association—maternal succor and carnal love—meets in Boucher's portrait of Madame de Pompadour at her dressing table.

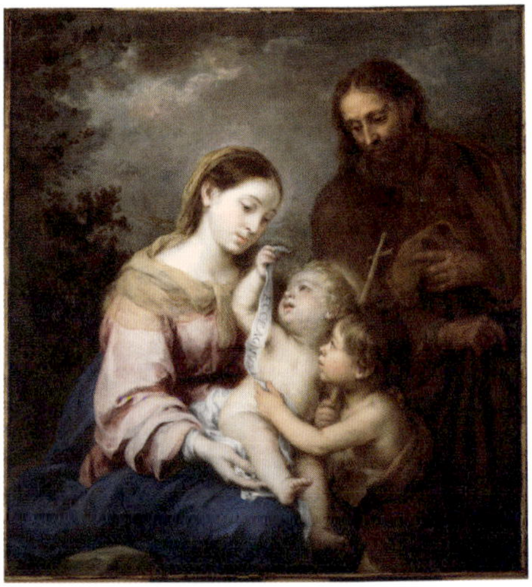

Fig. 1
Bartolomé Esteban Murillo, *Holy Family with Infant Saint John*, c. 1670. Oil on canvas, 120 × 110.5 cm. Harvard Art Museums/Fogg Museum, Bequest of Nettie G. Naumburg, 1930.189.

The fact that *Pompadour at Her Toilette* (see p. 16) ended up at Harvard is in some ways surprising. The only painting by Boucher in the museums' collections, it arrived as part of a group of works given by Charles E. Dunlap, a Harvard alumnus who had begun collecting eighteenth-century art under the influence of his uncle. Dunlap's taste differed from that of earlier Harvard donors of European paintings, such as Grenville L. Winthrop,

1. Edmond de Goncourt and Jules de Goncourt, *L'art du XVIIIe siècle*, vol. 1 (Paris: Charpentier, 1881), 243.

2. Critics leveled this charge both in Boucher's lifetime and more recently. We know about the former not from period sources but from defensive essays written by Abbé Le Blanc and Abbé Gougenot, supporters of the artist. Alastair Laing, *François Boucher, 1703–1770* (New York: Metropolitan Museum of Art, 1986), 239.

whose interest in French painting began with the more austere works of the Revolutionary period.[3] Perhaps it makes sense that eighteenth-century French painting, often derided as feminine and frivolous, had not previously been a collecting priority for the Fogg Museum: when Dunlap gifted *Pompadour at Her Toilette* in 1966, Harvard was still a male-dominated institution. The following year, Lamont Library, the main study space on campus and a social hub for undergraduates, agreed to give access to female graduate students at the university as well as undergraduates at Radcliffe College for the first time—on a trial basis.[4] Women did not begin living in Harvard dormitories until 1972. We do not know where the painting hung when it first arrived at the Fogg, but by 1970 it was installed in the office of Agnes Mongan, then serving as the first female director of the museum.[5] It is doubtful that a work of art considered to be the collection's greatest masterpiece—and indeed it is a significant work—would be sequestered in the office of even the most powerful museum director. Thus we can extrapolate that *Pompadour at Her Toilette* was not so easily integrated into the larger Fogg collection at first.

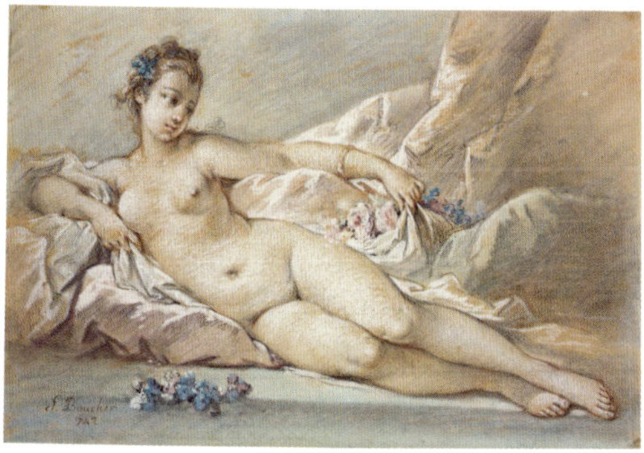

Fig. 2
François Boucher, *Reclining Nude*, 1742. Colored chalk on tan paper, 26 × 39 cm. Harvard Art Museums/Fogg Museum, Gift of Therese Kuhn Straus in memory of her husband, Herbert N. Straus, Harvard Class of 1903, 1978.59.

In fact, the work is unique not only within Harvard's collections, but among other French paintings from the period. Sitting at her toilette, or dressing table, Pompadour gazes directly at the viewer; prior to this depiction, no other known painting had portrayed a woman at her dressing table making such proud, unbroken eye contact. She is also the first known sitter to be shown applying makeup. At the time of its rediscovery, by composer and writer Maurice Vaucaire, in the early twentieth century, the painting was

3. Alvin L. Clark, Jr., *"To Delight the Eye": French Drawings and Paintings from the Collection of Charles E. Dunlap* (Cambridge, Mass.: Harvard University Art Museums, 2005).

4. Marcia B. Kline, "Lamont Will Open to Cliffies after Twenty Celibate Years," *Harvard Crimson*, December 8, 1966, https://www.thecrimson.com/article/1966/12/8/lamont-will-open-to-cliffies-after.

5. In a November 24, 1970, memo to Betty Jones, head of conservation at the Fogg, Mongan noted, "[Y]ou and I should have a session about the Madame de Pompadour hanging in my office." Mongan also first raised the issue of cleaning and relining the painting, in a memo to Jones on January 14, 1969. The memos are in the Harvard Art Museums Archives.

described as a “wonderful work,” “the adorable image of the favorite,” and “a magic portrait.”[6] It has since appeared in numerous exhibitions about Pompadour and on the cover of many books. While the iconography of the painting and the circumstances of its creation (and revision) have been discussed elsewhere, this is the first study of the portrait to focus on color.

Indeed, this project was initially conceived of as a full-scale exhibition about the use of and associations with the color pink in eighteenth- and nineteenth-century European art. Original aspirations, however, evolved over the course of 2020–21, eventually settling into the contours of the volume you hold in your hands: a focused reexamination of *Pompadour at Her Toilette* through the lens of color—pink in particular. New currents in scholarship and in the world at large made the time ripe for a fresh look at this remarkable painting and its sitter. In this endeavor, I am joined by three art historians, each of whom brings his or her unique research interests to the project. Mark Ledbury, Power Professor of Art History and Visual Culture and director of the Power Institute at the University of Sydney, has worked to rehabilitate Boucher’s reputation as a serious artist. In his essay in this volume, Ledbury detects intellectual rigor and powers of observation in Boucher’s references to the colors and forms of the natural world. Gabriella Szalay, the former Renke B. and Pamela M. Thye Curatorial Fellow in the Busch-Reisinger Museum, came to the Harvard Art Museums to study German porcelain while this project was still in its early stages. Here, she traces the history of colored porcelain to demonstrate how elements of the Pompadour portrait nod to the connection between the medium and the marquise. And Oliver Wunsch, an assistant professor of art history at Boston College whose research considers art’s role in the construction of race, explores the painting from this critical and timely point of view. I thank all three for their contributions and for helping me develop my own thinking about *Pompadour at Her Toilette*.

6. Maurice Vaucaire, “Un portrait inconnu de la Marquise de Pompadour par François Boucher,” *L’Illustration* 40 (1913): n.p.

I also wish to thank Heather Linton, curatorial assistant for special exhibitions and publications, for her commitment to this project as it changed over time. Further gratitude is owed to Micah Buis and Sarah Kuschner for guiding and editing this publication, to Zak Jensen for coordinating the design process, and to the team at IN-FO.CO, including Adam Michaels and Marina Kitchen, for the brilliant design. Miriam Stewart, Elizabeth Rudy, Meg Grasselli, Jessie Park, and especially Sophie Lynford—all current or former colleagues in the Division of European and American Art—supported this project in various ways, for which I am grateful. I extend my thanks to Francine Flynn and Elie Glyn for their early efforts toward, respectively, pursuing loans of artwork and creating preliminary exhibition designs, before the project changed shape and size. Chief curator Soyoung Lee helped mold the project through many discussions, and director Martha Tedeschi and deputy director Maureen Donovan provided much-needed institutional muscle to make this book a possibility. Thank you also to my curatorial colleague in the Division of Modern and Contemporary Art, Lynette Roth, whose shared appreciation for eighteenth-century German porcelain led the publication down paths I could not have imagined. In addition, I am grateful to Yuriko Jackall for discussions about color in the eighteenth century, and to Lucy Soutter and Lucy Peltz for talking through this project with me on more than one occasion, both in London and by phone. Thank you to Gillian Forrester, Tim Barringer, and the anonymous reviewers for the journal *Eighteenth-Century Studies* for reading earlier pieces of writing on this topic.

My dear husband Victor Agran helped and supported me while I was immersed in the worlds of Pompadour and pink. Xavier and Nico, I'm sorry I missed the trip to Six Flags Magic Mountain! I love all three of you and appreciate you so much.

A. Cassandra Albinson
Margaret S. Winthrop Curator of European Art
Head of the Division of European and American Art
Harvard Art Museums

The Color of Love

Pink and Sensibility in *Pompadour at Her Toilette*

A. Cassandra Albinson

IN MARCH 1938, AFTER THE ANNEXATION of Austria by Nazi Germany, Baron Louis von Rothschild (1882–1955), a member of the Austrian Jewish aristocracy, was taken into Nazi custody. While imprisoned, his property was confiscated by order of Arthur Seyss-Inquart, Hitler's recent appointee as leader of Austria. Among the items seized were paintings, including, possibly, François Boucher's *Pompadour at Her Toilette* (see p. 16).[1] Following the German surrender in 1945, Rothschild was reunited with a number of works from his collection, and in 1952, his cousin, Baron Maurice de Rothschild, sold the Pompadour portrait through New York dealer Rosenberg & Stiebel to an American collector with ties to Harvard.

This was not the first time in its history that the Pompadour portrait underwent movement and transition. The work was likely changing hands from its earliest years, although a lack of documentation makes it difficult to trace its exact path. It was perhaps gifted by the sitter, Jeanne-Antoinette Poisson, Marquise de Pompadour, to her brother, Abel-François Poisson de Vandières, Marquis de Marigny, who may have sent it

1. While a complete list of the confiscated property has yet to be found, period accounts of the seizure, which happened days after Rothschild's arrest, describe the removal of valuables from his Vienna residence as exhaustive. SS officers were seen exiting the home with "gold framed picture[s]," silver, and "other loot." Quoted in Lynn H. Nicholas, *The Rape of Europa: The Fate of Europe's Treasures in the Third Reich and the Second World War* (New York: Knopf Doubleday Publishing Group, 2009), 39. Given Hitler's documented fondness for Boucher and for the artist's portraits of Madame de Pompadour in particular, it is assumed that the Harvard painting was included in Rothschild's impounded collection. See Giles MacDonogh, *1938: Hitler's Gamble* (New York: Basic Books, 2009), 137; and Niall Ferguson, *The House of Rothschild: The World's Banker, 1849–1999* (New York: Viking, 1999), 471, 477.

back to Boucher so the artist could make additions to his composition before returning it to Marigny. (The portrait was included in a 1781 inventory of Marigny's estate.[2]) It is also possible that the painting remained with Pompadour and was gifted to her brother at a later date, sometime before the marquise's death in 1764. A mistress of Louis XV of France, Pompadour was not a member of the royal family, and since her portraits were therefore not national property, they could be passed to her kin. However, Boucher's painting is probably not indicated in the posthumous inventory of her possessions, suggesting that Marigny acquired it during Pompadour's lifetime.[3] It is likely that the Boucher portrait left Marigny's estate soon after his own death in 1781.[4] It may have departed France not long after, as it disappeared from records in the period between the listing in Marigny's inventory and the early twentieth century. In 1906, Albert von Rothschild loaned the painting to an exhibition in Vienna, where it was attributed to Jean-Marc Nattier, and in 1913, it was celebrated (as by Boucher) in a magazine article about Rothschild's collection. The painting's peripatetic existence and the mystery of its early years is but one reason why it continues to capture the imagination of scholars and the public alike.

This volume takes up several key questions that illuminate understudied or, in some cases, wholly unexplored aspects of Pompadour's likeness, highlighting in particular the interplay between Boucher's portrait of the famous marquise and the contemporary fashion for, and changing notions of, the color pink. In the essays that follow, Mark Ledbury offers a new reading of the painting and a deeper understanding of Boucher's approach to portraiture as inspired by the fecundity and colors of the natural world, particularly shells and sea life.

2. The transcribed and translated 1781 *Inventory of the Estate of the Marquis de Marigny et de Menars Proces Verbal d'Inventaire 1er juin 1781 après le décès de Monsieur le Marquis de [Marigny et de] Menars* places the painting (no. 1042) in the Galerie of the Hôtel de Menars. See this document in Alden R. Gordon, *The Houses and Collections of the Marquis de Marigny*, ed. Carolyne Ayçaguer-Ron (Los Angeles: Getty Publications, 2003), 317.

3. For a partial transcription of Pompadour's inventory, see Jean Cordey, *Inventaire des biens de Madame de Pompadour rédigé après son décès* (Paris: La Société des Bibliophiles François, 1939). See note 26, below, for a source on how portraits were inventoried in eighteenth-century France.

4. The painting was not included in Marigny's posthumous estate sale in 1782. See F. Basan and F. Ch. Joullain, *Catalogue des différens objets de curiosités dans les sciences et arts: Qui composoient le cabinet de feu M. le Marquis de Menars, commandeur des ordres du roi...* (Paris: Basan, 1782).

Gabriella Szalay writes about Pompadour's affinities for porcelain and pink, placing the latter in the context of porcelain production across Europe in the mid-eighteenth century. And finally, Oliver Wunsch approaches the painting from the perspective of race to demonstrate how debates over skin tone—and white privilege in particular—are embedded in Boucher's portrait.

My discussion focuses on the painting's iconography as it relates to issues of sensibility, familial relationships, and maternity, and the ways in which pink signaled those concerns to Pompadour and Boucher as well as their contemporaries. A singular yet highly influential figure at court, Pompadour strove to represent herself as enmeshed in intimate relationships, most obviously with the king. Her role as a mother, however, was necessarily less overt, and as a result this aspect of her life has gone largely unexamined.

Historiography of the Harvard Portrait

One of the most famous portraits of the eighteenth century, *Pompadour at Her Toilette* has been the subject of numerous studies over the past two decades.[5] It became known to the public in 1966, upon coming to Harvard's Fogg Museum as part of a larger gift of eighteenth-century French art donated by Charles E. Dunlap. In 2002, Xavier Salmon, curator at Versailles, staged the exhibition *Madame de Pompadour et les Arts*, the culmination of years of research into Pompadour's role as a patron of the arts. The Harvard painting traveled with the show to Paris, Munich, and London and was featured in the accompanying catalogue.[6] That same year, Alden Gordon and Teri Hensick published a groundbreaking technical essay that re-dated the portrait from 1758 to 1750 (on which more below).[7] The possibility of an

5. A good introduction to the controversies surrounding the creation, iconography, and dating of the portrait is Humphrey Wine's entry in Xavier Salmon, *Madame de Pompadour et les Arts* (Paris: Réunion des musées nationaux, 2002), 152–54, no. 30.

6. Ibid.

7. Alden R. Gordon and Teri Hensick, "The Picture within the Picture: Boucher's 1750 Portrait of Madame de Pompadour Identified," *Apollo* 155 (480) (February 2002): 21–30. The authors noted that the date and signature appear, after analysis, to be later additions to the painting, added well after Boucher's and Pompadour's lifetimes.

iteration that predated the completed painting was theorized as early as 1977, however, when Eunice Williams noted during a conservation treatment at the Fogg that there were visible seams on the back of the canvas, which was not yet lined. Williams hypothesized that the painting was originally a small rectangle that was later enlarged to an oval format.[8]

The portrait has been a touchstone for feminist art criticism because of its iconography and coloring. Writing on the work of impressionist painter Berthe Morisot, Anne Higonnet and Tamar Garb introduced the idea that a scene of a woman making herself up at her toilette could be interpreted as a meditation on the nature of painting.[9] In 1987, Jacqueline Lichtenstein published her seminal essay "Making Up Representation: The Risks of Femininity," which does not deal directly with artistic representations of women wearing makeup but points out the powerful comparisons drawn between cosmetics and color in painting from academic discourses of the seventeenth century—directly before Boucher's time. The metaphor was used to advance accusations of artifice: makeup, like courtesans, provided "fugitive pleasures" that could confuse and overwhelm the viewer/lover.[10] The Harvard painting first entered this discussion the same year, in an essay by Elise Goodman-Soellner, who later included her article in a book on portraits of Pompadour.[11] In 2000, Melissa Hyde examined the portrait through the lens of Boucher's efforts to establish an artistic identity in eighteenth-century Paris, drawing attention to the fact that his work was decried by many contemporaries as superficial, especially because of his overuse of the color pink.[12] Hyde also explored the painting as a kind of self-portrait of the sitter, crafted through the hand of Boucher.[13] The next year, in a crucial step, Ewa Lajer-Burcharth

8. See the letter from Eunice Williams to Marianne Roland Michel and Jeanne Cailleux dated March 16, 1977, in the object file at the Harvard Art Museums.

9. Tamar Garb, *The Painted Face: Portraits of Women in France, 1814–1914* (New Haven, Conn.: Yale University Press, 2007), 8–9; and Anne Higonnet, *Berthe Morisot's Images of Women* (Cambridge, Mass.: Harvard University Press, 1992), 169.

10. Jacqueline Lichtenstein, "Making Up Representation: The Risks of Femininity," *Representations* 20 (Fall 1987): 77–87, esp. 82.

11. Elise Goodman-Soellner, "Boucher's *Madame de Pompadour at Her Toilette*," *Simiolus* 17 (1) (1987): 41–58; and Elise Goodman-Soellner, *The Portraits of Madame de Pompadour: Celebrating the Femme Savante* (Berkeley: University of California Press, 2000). The Harvard portrait appealed to Goodman-Soellner's larger interest in Renaissance paintings of women at their toilette, and her work helps situate Boucher's work within this broader iconographic tradition, contextualizing the portrait of Pompadour alongside earlier images of French royal mistresses.

12. Melissa Hyde, "The 'Makeup' of the Marquise: Boucher's Portrait of Pompadour at Her Toilette," *The Art Bulletin* 82 (3) (September 2000): 455.

13. Hyde notes that Pompadour's brush is closer to the ribbon at her throat than to her cheeks: "It seems to imply that her hand authored the bow as well, and perhaps by extension, the entire image"; ibid., 464.

challenged readers to "consider a patron [Pompadour] not as a mere factor or an external circumstance of artistic production but as an internal, pictorial effect."[14] She argued that the inclusion of the bracelet with a cameo of Louis XV "introduces another actor in the haptic arena of Pompadour's self-definition: the king." For Lajer-Burcharth, the trope of Pompadour applying makeup "combined the painter's and the patroness's touch," thereby implying "*interchangeability* between her act and the painter's act of portrayal."[15] A professor in Harvard's Department of History of Art and Architecture, Lajer-Burcharth has used the painting extensively in her teaching, guaranteeing its continued relevance to future specialists in eighteenth-century French art.

Through these writings, the Pompadour portrait became a key object in the feminist project of realigning the study of art from the visual to the haptic. In emphasizing the agency of the marquise, Hyde and Lajer-Burcharth also reintroduced Pompadour as not only a patron of great artists, but an artistic actor herself. Hyde and, more recently, Susan Wager have taken into consideration Pompadour's printmaking as a means to further explore the idea of the sitter as artist of her own image.[16] The essays in the present volume build on the work of these scholars, all of whom respond in some way to an earlier critic's argument that Pompadour's clout was overstated, that she was more of a consumer than a creator or influencer.[17]

Much of Pompadour's current and historical notoriety comes from the fact that her power derived in large measure from her position as official mistress of Louis XV—and therefore from her sexual relationship with the king.[18] This relationship is critical to the visual argument of the Harvard painting. Appearing alone and in perfect self-possession, she meets the viewer's gaze, although her

14. Ewa Lajer-Burcharth, "Pompadour's Touch: Difference in Representation," *Representations* 73 (1) (Winter 2001): 55.

15. Ibid., 70, 74.

16. Hyde, "The 'Makeup' of the Marquise," 463–64; and Susan M. Wager, "The Fast and the Fugitive: Pompadour's Curatorial Self/Portrait at Versailles," *Journal18* 8 (Fall 2019); available at http://www.journal18.org/41162. There is an impression of Pompadour's suite of engravings, *Suite d'estampes gravées par madame de Pompadour d'après les pierres gravées de Guay*, in Harvard's Houghton Library.

17. Donald Posner, "Mme. de Pompadour as a Patron of Visual Arts," *The Art Bulletin* 72 (1) (March 1990): 74–105. For a reassessment of Pompadour's patronage, see Mark Ledbury, "Patronage," in *The Oxford Handbook of the Ancien Régime*, ed. William Doyle (Oxford: Oxford University Press, 2011).

18. For the ways that Pompadour has been discussed (and slandered) in literature, see Alden Gordon, "Searching for the Elusive Madame de Pompadour," *Eighteenth-Century Studies* 37 (1) (Fall 2003): 91–111; and Pamela J. Warner, "*Madame de Pompadour et les arts*, Musée national des châteaux de Versailles et de Trianon, 14 février–19 mai 2002," *Cahiers Edmond et Jules de Goncourt* 1 (9) (2002): 283–85.

glance is shifted a few degrees off-center, so that the sitter maintains a slight air of remove. There is a mirror to her left on the table, and the position of Pompadour's head and hands suggests that she has momentarily looked away from its reflective surface, as if distracted from the act of applying her rouge by the presence of the artist/viewer. We catch her not at the beginning of her beauty ritual but in the process of putting on the final touches: her cheeks are already heavily colored with several tones of pink. Pompadour's proximity to the viewer and the waist-up view, with arms and face situated frontally, will seem natural to modern viewers familiar with the posture of the "selfie." Part intimate self-portrait, part public projection, a selfie can be shared privately with another person or posted to image-sharing platforms for wider consumption. The Harvard painting, I argue, likewise served a dual function; a private talisman on one hand, it also presented a more public depiction of Pompadour as consciously enacting bonded, affective feelings for those individuals closest to her.

The expression of these ostensibly more private feelings, and of the concept of sensibility as it was understood in the eighteenth century, does not negate the overall importance of *Pompadour at Her Toilette* within the marquise's attempts to fashion her public image. In fact, it may reinforce the painting's central role in her personal iconography, because Pompadour's position was predicated on connections and relationships defined by sexual and familial bonds.[19] The work was part of a larger cultural shift in France, where sensitivity and feeling based on family affection and private bonding were assuming dominance in the public expression of emotions.[20]

In their 2002 study, Gordon and Hensick affirmed that the first, much

19. Alastair Laing has written: "We know virtually none of the portraits of Mme de Pompadour from either contemporary reports or engravings; they led a very private existence in the apartments of herself and her circle." See Alastair Laing, *François Boucher, 1703–1770* (New York: Metropolitan Museum of Art, 1986), 254. I would argue, however, that her position at court and the public-facing roles of relatives such as Marigny and Lenormant de Tournehem meant that any image of Pompadour had a wider reach than other "personal" portraits inside aristocratic apartments at Versailles or other châteaux. Alden Gordon has made a similar assertion, noting that "[Pompadour's] apartments at Versailles were effectively France's most elite salon." See Alden R. Gordon, "The Dispersal of the Estate of Madame de Pompadour: New Documentary Evidence," *Burlington Magazine* 148 (1238) (May 2006): 312.

20. For an overview of the "remarkable consensus among the educated elite about the centrality to virtue of natural sentiment" in mid-eighteenth-century France, see William M. Reddy, "Sentimentalism and Its Erasure: The Role of Emotions in the Era of the French Revolution," *The Journal of Modern History* 72 (1) (March 2000): 124.

smaller iteration of the Harvard portrait was a rectangular composition depicting only Pompadour's head, shoulders, and hands, not the dressing table or mirror. This aligns with the description of a painting in letters from Pompadour to her brother in 1750, leading Gordon and Hensick to argue that the marquise sent the Harvard portrait to Marigny in Italy that year as a gift, a badge of his sister's high position that he could display in his chambers. The hypothesis, now debated, called into question what stage of life Pompadour was in when the painting was created, with important implications for scholarly interpretations since 2002.[21] By dating the nucleus of the portrait as early as 1750 and contending that in its smaller iteration it traveled to Rome, Gordon and Hensick downplay the importance of the toilette scene, including the application of rouge (as well as at least some of the portrait of Louis XV on the bracelet), all of which, they argue, must have been added by Boucher at the request of Pompadour's brother after the painting came into Marigny's possession and returned with him to Paris. Gordon and Hensick surmise that the changes were made in large part to hide damage to the canvas incurred in transit from Rome to Paris.[22] While inspired by the ingenuity of this carefully researched hypothesis, the present essay pursues a more fluid interpretation of the timeline, maximizing the angles of approach to see what new insights

21. Gordon and Hensick, "The Picture within the Picture," 22. They quote letters from *Marquise de Pompadour Correspondence avec son père, M. Poisson et son frère, M. de Vandières* (Paris: J. Baur, 1870), 37. The letter describing the painting is translated and annotated by Laing in a catalogue entry on a sketch of Pompadour at the spinet, now in the Louvre, as follows: "I shall take great care not to send you my portraits by Liotard, but I am going to send you the copy of one done by Boucher, which is charming, and which [the original, not the copy, as her subsequent letter of 15 June makes clear] he will finish from me." See Laing, *François Boucher, 1703–1770*, 252. Jo Hedley has noted that the idea the second portrait would be finished "from" Pompadour (that is, with the sitter present) indicates that there was a fair amount of imagination that went into some of Boucher's portraits of Pompadour. Jo Hedley, *François Boucher: Seductive Visions* (London: Wallace Collection, 2004), 100.

22. See Gordon and Hensick, "The Picture within the Picture," 21–30. Laing questioned this restrictive dating in his essay "Madame de Pompadour et les enfants de Boucher," in Salmon, *Madame de Pompadour et les Arts*, 42. For more on this debate, see Melissa Hyde, *Making Up the Rococo: François Boucher and His Critics*, Texts & Documents (Los Angeles: Getty Research Institute, 2006), 117.

23. Many scholars who accept the visible signature and date of 1758 have used it to argue that the portrait was created to counter rumors of Pompadour's ill-health that year and to insist on her continued beauty and fecundity. See, for instance, Lajer-Burcharth, "Pompadour's Touch," 70; and Goodman-Soellner, "Boucher's *Madame de Pompadour at Her Toilette*," 41–42. Until the Gordon and Hensick essay cast doubt on the signature, there was little reason to think that it was fake. For a possible dating of the portrait to around 1754–55, see Humphrey Wine's entry on the portrait in Salmon, *Madame de Pompadour et les Arts*, 154. Again, a definitive dating is in some ways beside the point in terms of our overall understanding of the work, as I hope the essays in this volume will show.

may spring up.[23] We know that the portrait was in Pompadour's family orbit; whether commissioned or ordered changed and enlarged by Marigny or the marquise herself, its iconography must hold valuable clues about how she and her family members understood Pompadour's social position and relationships—and how they used pink to tell that story.

Pompadour as Outsider

Key to understanding Pompadour's relationships is the name we know her by. Her unique situation is evident in the fact that, contrary to general practice for women of the time, she was and is referred to only by last name. The official mistress of Louis XV for twenty years, Pompadour drew power from a powerful man, but she also stood apart from him in social status and name and in her literal and figurative position at French court. Pompadour was the title given to her by the king; it was not a family name associated with her husband or father, nor was it attached to Louis himself, who was not her spouse.[24] By calling her Pompadour, we insist on her singularity: there was no Madame de Pompadour before her elevation in 1745, and there would not be another after her death nineteen years later. Even if Pompadour's daughter, Alexandrine d'Étiolles, had lived to adulthood, she would not have inherited the title. This identity, solely her own, gave Pompadour fame, fortune, and power, but it also meant that she was different—and alone.

As a young wife, Pompadour was known as Madame d'Étiolles. She gave birth to two children: a boy who died in infancy and Alexandrine, who lived only until the age of ten. Pompadour is often said to have come from a lowly background, and it is true she was not born into court society, but her family in fact belonged to a newly affluent class who amassed their wealth by selling provisions to the French army. She was well educated at home, and before

24. Her full title was Jeanne-Antoinette Poisson, Duchesse, Marquise de Pompadour et de Menars, Dame de Noizieux, Saint-Uuen et autres lieux, l'une des Dames du palais de la Reyne, Épouse séparée de Mre Charles Guillaume Lenormant, Chevalier; see Colin Bailey, "Madame de Pompadour," *The Burlington Magazine* 145 (1204) (July 2003): 229. Bailey quotes Cordey, *Inventaire des biens de Madame de Pompadour rédigé après son décès*, 1. Pompadour was the name of an extinct family from the eponymous area in central France, whose estate was the king's prerogative to grant.

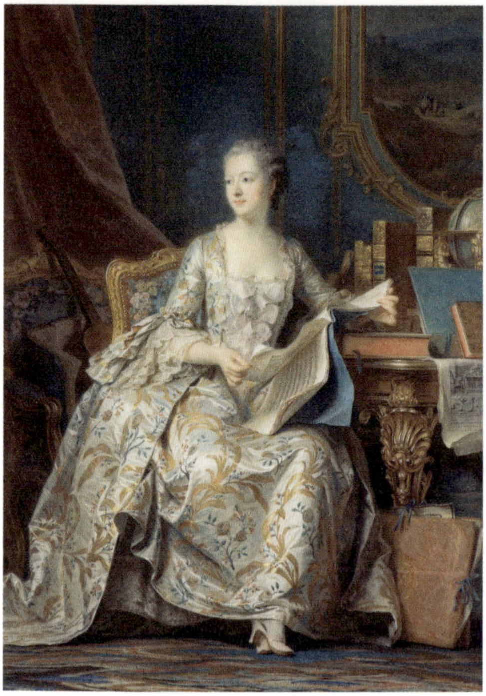

Fig. 1
Maurice-Quentin de La Tour, *Full-Length Portrait of the Marquise de Pompadour*, 1752–55. Pastel on gray-blue paper with gouache highlights; face cut out and mounted to paper, 177.5 × 131 cm. Musée du Louvre, Paris, INV 27614.

her affair with Louis XV, Madame d'Étiolles had already been acquainted with writers and artists such as Montesquieu, Cochin, Voltaire, and Boucher. It is believed that her physical love affair with the king lasted only five years, from 1745 to 1750, but this is impossible to know for sure. No matter the length of the sexual relationship, Pompadour maintained her name, titles, and apartments at Versailles until her death. She was also forever severed from her previous life upon becoming the king's official mistress. Unlike the queen, Marie Leszczyńska, Pompadour was not surrounded by courtiers, and while Leszczyńska bore ten children (seven of whom lived to adulthood), the marquise was often separated from her daughter, who spent most of her short life away from Versailles. Pompadour did have her brother with her at court, in addition to other powerful male supporters, but her anomalous position brought with it a certain degree of isolation.

Only two major portraits of Pompadour were exhibited publicly during her lifetime: one at the Paris Salon of 1755, the other in 1757. (In total, about eleven painted portraits of Pompadour from her lifetime survive today.) As far as we know, the Harvard portrait was never exhibited while Pompadour was alive.[25] She probably commissioned both of the exhibited portraits, as they were thought to have been in her possession at the time of her death. The Harvard portrait, on the other hand, does not appear to have been retained by Pompadour, although the idiosyncrasies of how portraits were inventoried in France make it impossible to say for certain.[26] The portrait exhibited in 1755, a life-sized pastel by Maurice-Quentin de La Tour, focuses primarily on Pompadour as musician, lover of the theater, and performer, but examination reveals that her literary interests and dedication to craftsmanship

25. Two works depicting Pompadour as a sultana were also exhibited at the 1755 Salon; while critics recognized the figures to be Pompadour, the paintings were not exhibited as official portraits. See Perrin Stein, "Madame de Pompadour and the Harem Imagery at Bellevue," *Gazette des Beaux-Arts*, ser. 6, 136 (123) (January 1994): 29–44. See also Oliver Wunsch's essay.

26. See Gordon, *The Houses and Collections of the Marquis de Marigny*, 317. Because portraits were considered family chattel, not works to be priced for possible sale, the descriptions in Pompadour's posthumous inventory make the works extremely difficult to identify with exactitude.

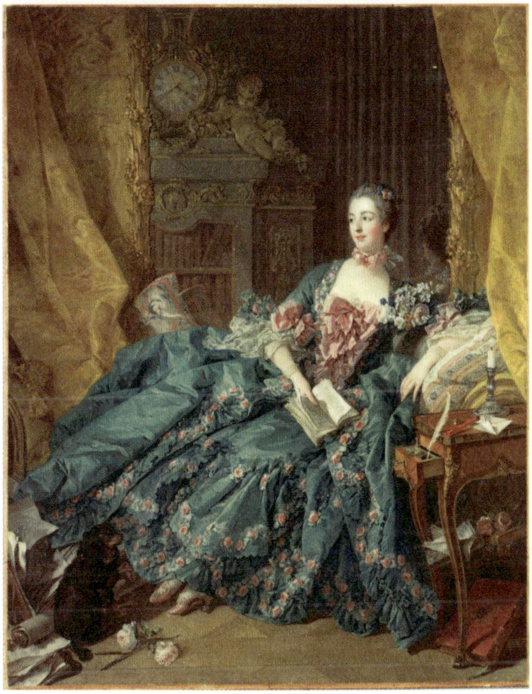

Fig. 2
François Boucher, *Madame de Pompadour*, 1756. Oil on canvas, 205 × 161 cm. Alte Pinakothek, Munich, HUW 18.

are also represented (Fig. 1). There is a guitar nestled in the chair behind her, and she holds a musical score in her lap. While her head is turned away from us, her alert posture, crossed feet, and active arms and hands—as well as the way she is brightly lit—suggest that Pompadour is perhaps preparing to sing. One of the bound volumes is identifiable as Voltaire's book on Henry IV, an earlier king of France seen as a model for Louis XV. The spine of a volume of Diderot's *Encyclopédie* is also visible, as is *Traité des pierres gravées* (Treaty on Engraved Gems) by Pierre-Jean Mariette. Together, these publications indicate Pompadour's dedication to modern learning and classification, collecting (especially of the cameos that she had begun to devote herself to), and a salon-like culture of discussion and debate. The choice of La Tour as artist and the selected medium (pastel) are also significant: La Tour had created one of the most famous pastels of Louis XV about a decade earlier, and in repeating the medium here, connects the king and his mistress through portraiture.

A year later, Boucher responded to the celebrated La Tour painting with his own large portrait of Pompadour (Fig. 2). Like La Tour, Boucher had previously worked for the king: in 1736, the artist was one of nine commissioned to paint exotic hunting scenes for the monarch's petit appartements at Versailles.[27] In his portrait of Pompadour, Boucher depicted the king's mistress in a more private setting and in a contemplative rather than scholarly or performative mode, but the position of her head, with her gaze drifting off to the right, is remarkably similar to that in La Tour's. The clock reflected in the mirror indicates the setting is

27. David Wakefield, *Boucher* (London: Chaucer Press, 2005), 66.

afternoon, and Pompadour wears an elaborate dress suited for an official event at the court of Versailles. Alastair Laing connected this portrait's creation and exhibition to Pompadour's ascension to the position of lady-in-waiting to the queen that year.[28] A shelf of books is reflected in the mirror, but we cannot read any of the titles, nor can we make out the text she has open on her lap. In the left corner, sheet music and an engraving that Pompadour made after Boucher's drawn copy of a gem carved by one of her favorite artists, Jacques Guay, reference her own artistry and ongoing support of both Boucher and Guay. The crossed roses in the foreground may subtly allude to Pompadour's love match with the king, yet in this portrait she is attended only by her faithful dog, Mimi. The quill, letter, and sealing wax to her left suggest possible correspondence with someone far away, contributing to the painting's air of solitude. During her time with Louis XV, Pompadour worked to establish a reputation as one both worthy of a position at court (as the queen's lady-in-waiting) and fundamentally removed from the intrigue. This portrait enacts that balance by showing Pompadour in courtly costume in a rich interior suggestive of Versailles, but in a private apartment instead of the grand enfilades, swathed in protective curtains ready to close off the scene to our viewing.[29]

The two portraits of Pompadour exhibited in the sitter's lifetime depict her as accomplished—as possessing intellect, artistic talent, courtly composure—but also quite alone. Unlike portraits of the queen, which typically include an image of the king (often a bust on display on a shelf or pedestal nearby), the only references in Pompadour's public portraits are to herself: in each, her personal shield (a cartouche surrounding three towers) appears in lieu of a representation of another person. In the La Tour portrait, the shield can be seen on a leather portfolio at her feet,

28. Laing, *François Boucher, 1703–1770*, 267.

29. Pompadour's association with respite from court grew in part from her involvement in a number of garden pavilion projects at various castles where the king could take a break from the rigors of court protocol, the most famous being the Petit Trianon at Versailles. On these, see Meredith Martin, *Dairy Queens: The Politics of Pastoral Architecture from Catherine de' Medici to Marie-Antoinette* (Cambridge, Mass.: Harvard University Press, 2011), 114–57. One of Pompadour's great gifts was cultivating supporters, and she seems to have been close to her brother, but her existence also appears to have been isolated at times. The larger portrait of Pompadour by Boucher now in Munich was created two years after the death of her only surviving child, when Pompadour was navigating the choppy waters of court very much alone. See Katie Scott, "Framing Ambition: The Interior Politics of Madame de Pompadour," *Art History* 28 (2) (May 2005): 253. Scott writes of the Munich painting: "Circumscribed, ultimately then, as her place, Pompadour sits in her tower daydreaming about her desire for status and autonomy."

and in the Boucher painting, it is inscribed as decoration on the bookcase. The circuit of solitary reflection is unbroken by the presence or suggestion of another.

Picturing Intimacy

The Harvard portrait, conversely, insists on links to the king rather than separation from him. Critical to this connection is the presentation of Pompadour in the act of applying rouge, a visible means of preparation for her lover. The painting is also the only instance within Pompadour's personal iconography that contains an image of the king. Often seen in profile on coins and in prints in France, Louis XV would have been easily recognizable to any viewer of this portrait. Boucher's rendering was probably inspired by a cameo carved by Guay from a sardonyx stone with three distinct colors, the most dramatic of which provides the inky, blackish background (Fig. 3).[30] Inset into surrounds of diamonds and emeralds fashioned by jeweler Pierre-André Jacquemin into a garland and bows, the surviving cameo and its pair (representing Henry IV) likely belonged to Pompadour.[31] The radical change to its background color in the Harvard portrait—from black to a pink that matches the bows on Pompadour's dress and the rouge on her cheeks—was probably an imaginative and aesthetic move on Boucher's part.

This emphasis on the color pink calls to mind Pompadour's and Louis XV's support of the Sèvres manufactory, royal producer of porcelain—the only artistic material aside from oil paint that could render pink

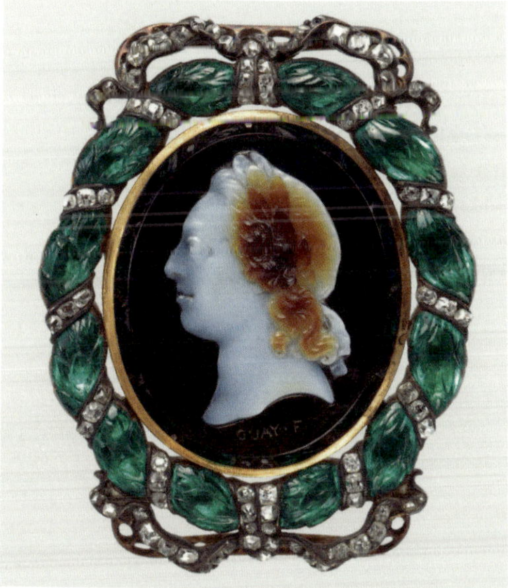

Fig. 3
Jacques Guay, *Louis XV Crowned with Laurels*, c. 1750. Sardonyx, emerald, and diamond, 45 × 35 mm. Bibliothèque nationale de France, IFN-55009770.

30. There are contemporaneous cameos in agate, which can be clear or translucid in parts, that are tinted on the back with red or rose to create a pinkish background. See, for example, Babelon 662 in the Cabinet des Médailles, Bibliothèque nationale de France. For more on cameos and color, see Mark Ledbury's essay in this volume.

31. See Salmon, *Madame de Pompadour et les Arts*, n. 113. However, neither is included in the list of cameos and carved gems that the marquise left to the king in 1764. See also Diana Scarisbrick, *Portrait Jewels: Opulence and Intimacy from the Medici to the Romanovs* (London: Thames and Hudson, 2011), 158–61.

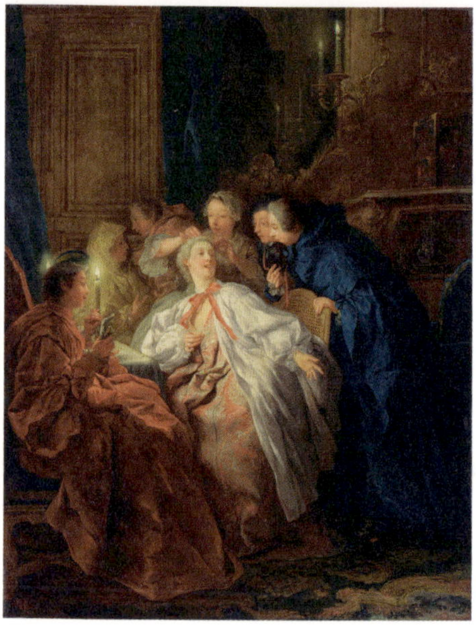

Fig. 4
Jean-François de Troy, *Before the Ball*, 1735. Oil on canvas, 83 × 65.4 cm. J. Paul Getty Museum, Los Angeles, 84.PA.668.

in such a pure, durable, and clear form in the eighteenth century. Pink binds Pompadour and Louis together, once more making them distorted mirrors or opposites of one another: while Pompadour's front-facing visage is flushed, Louis XV's face is pale and seen only in profile against a pink backdrop.[32] Janus-faced, they seem permanently joined.

The Harvard portrait is further distinguished from La Tour's pastel and Boucher's larger public portrait by the viewer's position relative to the marquise. We see the back of the mirror on the dressing table but not Pompadour's reflection in the mirror itself, intimating that we are seated directly across the table from her. The close physical proximity underscores the intimacy of what she is doing—of preparing herself for her lover, making herself pink in anticipation of him, and exhibiting to us, in detail, the bracelet with his portrait that she wears.[33] The La Tour portrait, by contrast, shows Pompadour's body pulled back into the picture plane and somewhat inaccessible to the viewer. Her legs, crossed at the ankles, and the large and floppy musical score on her lap allow her space of her own. The same is true of the full-length Boucher portrait, in which she seems to withdraw into the room. The mirror behind her reflects the back of her head and the chamber across from her, giving a sense of receding depth.

The toilette in the Harvard portrait takes on an intimacy and seriousness that is unlike earlier depictions of the setting as one filled with frivolity and convivial sociability. Pink was, by Pompadour's lifetime, the color of the toilette costume. In Jean-François de Troy's 1735 genre painting *Before the Ball* (Fig. 4), the central figure wears a white peignoir tied with a pink ribbon at her neck as she prepares to go out for the evening. The work is an early indication that it was generally understood that women's

32. Lajer-Burcharth has written eloquently on the importance of the king's portrait; see especially "Pompadour's Touch," 77–80.

33. For the connection between blushing and sexual arousal, see Angela Rosenthal, "Visceral Culture: Blushing and the Legibility of Whiteness in Eighteenth-Century British Portraiture," *Art History* 24 (4) (2004): 563–92; Aimée Marcereau DeGalan, "Lead White or Dead White? Dangerous Beauty Practices of Eighteenth-Century England," *Bulletin of the Detroit Institute of Arts* 76 (12) (2002): 38–49; and W. Ray Crozier, "The Blush: Literary and Psychological Perspectives," *Journal for the Theory of Social Behavior* 46 (4) (2016): 502–12.

peignoirs (worn to protect clothing from makeup and hair powder) most often featured pink ribbons. This combination of pink and white appears again and again in images of the dressing room post-1700, many of which portray a woman of wealth and taste getting ready to interact with the larger world at a ball or other social gathering.[34] Some depictions were satirical, as the visual trope was ripe for playing on the power of women to manipulate their environment, as well as for commentary on the frailty of vanity and the people who furnished the vanity of the very rich—dressers, spiritual advisors, music masters, jewelers, and more. Pompadour was clearly familiar with this particular realm of satire, for she owned Charles-Antoine Coypel's *Pleasures of Childhood; or, Child's Play during the Morning Toilet* (Fig. 5), in which rotund, half-naked, putti-like figures flutter around a seated child who holds a pot of rouge and applies it to her own cheek. This quasi-pornographic painting accentuates the comparatively serious way in which Pompadour presented herself and the unusual emphasis in the Harvard portrait on her intimacy with the king. Leaving out any frantic activity or doting behavior by others, Boucher depicts Pompadour alone, calmly preparing for her lover.

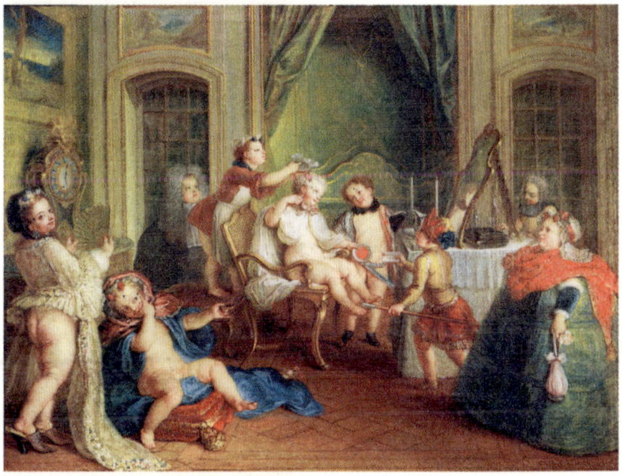

Fig. 5
Charles-Antoine Coypel, *Pleasures of Childhood; or, Child's Play during the Morning Toilet*, 1728. Oil on canvas, 65.7 × 83.2 cm. Collection of Dr. Martin L. Cohen, M.D., and Sharleen Cooper Cohen, Malibu.

Boucher's *A Lady on Her Day Bed*, now in the Frick Collection (Fig. 6), marks a shift toward the sense of enclosure and privacy that was becoming more the norm. Although painted seven years before Pompadour first sat for Boucher (and two years before she became Louis XV's mistress), *A Lady on Her Day Bed* was a touchstone for the artist's portrait of the marquise and is crucial to understanding the Harvard portrait. It is largely in relation to this earlier work that *Pompadour at Her Toilette* can be read as

34. Kimberly Chrisman-Campbell, "Dressing to Impress: The Morning Toilette and the Fabrication of Femininity," in *Paris: Life and Luxury in the Eighteenth Century*, ed. Charissa Bremer-David (Los Angeles: J. Paul Getty Museum, 2011), 53.

Fig. 6
François Boucher, *A Lady on Her Day Bed*, 1743. Oil on canvas, 57.2 × 68.3 cm. The Frick Collection, New York, 1937.1.139.

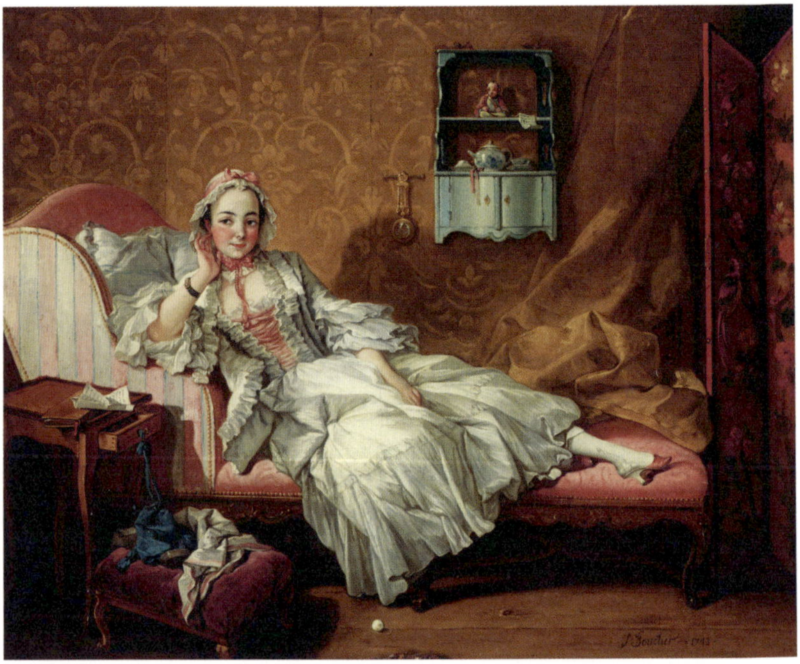

an image about intimacy rather than vanity. In both paintings, pink is a primary visual indicator of a strong and harmonious connection between man and woman: in the case of *A Lady on Her Day Bed*, between Boucher and his sitter (often said to be his wife, although this is disputed), and in the later work, between Pompadour and Louis XV. In the first, we see precursors to aspects of the Harvard portrait—the lady's blush, her hand held next to her cheek, pink ribbons, and the bracelet presumably holding a miniature portrait—despite the paintings' differences in size and technique as well as the gap between their creation dates.[35]

35. Colin Bailey, *The Age of Watteau, Chardin, and Fragonard: Masterpieces of French Genre Painting* (Ottowa: National Gallery of Canada, 2003), 224; and Colin Bailey, "Marie-Jeanne Buzeau, Madame Boucher," *The Burlington Magazine* 147 (1225) (April 2005): 224–34.

Maternal Pompadour

Pompadour in the Harvard portrait appears almost fixed in place by passages of blue and pink paint. A brilliant blue flower sits perfectly at the center of her head, and the composition is anchored by touches of pink: on her cheeks and lips (and even inside her nose), on the ribbon that encircles her neck, on the brush hovering to the right of that ribbon, and below the true center of the image, forming a shape reminiscent of an upside-down heart out of Pompadour's smooth, white upper chest. Her bodice is held in tension by more pink ribbons, and her arms appear almost bound to her sides by similar decorations at each elbow. Separated from these ribbons by only the thinnest strip of gold paint is the pink powder in Pompadour's rouge palette. Likewise, delicate rows of pearls and diamonds demarcate the pink surface of the cameo of Louis XV from the pink silk that surrounds it. The bottom row is more robust than the top, where the bracelet disappears into the ribbons above. The lowest of these pink ribbons is narrowly separated by white paint from the blue ribbon snaking across the surface of the dressing table.

The invention of pink as a very specific color of the highest fashion was an endeavor that Pompadour and Louis XV embarked on together, first and foremost as influential patrons of French porcelain. The crown's investment in "la porcelaine de France" as a tool of diplomatic power, a means of visually unifying French court, and a point of national pride that could compete with porcelain from the German states and from Asia began before Pompadour met the king. But in 1756, she was no doubt involved in advocating to move the royal factory to Sèvres, close to her château at Bellevue. Sèvres was at this time able to produce only what is called soft-paste porcelain; while weaker than hard-paste or "true" porcelain, soft-paste bodies could take on colors that would not adhere well to hard-paste wares (for more on this topic, see Gabriella Szalay's essay in this volume). Pink was the most famous

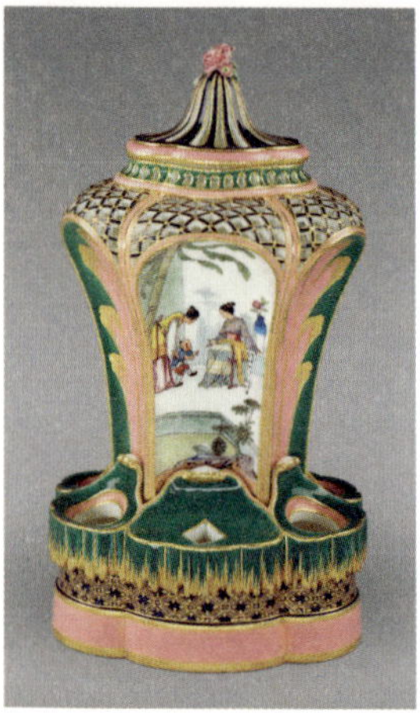
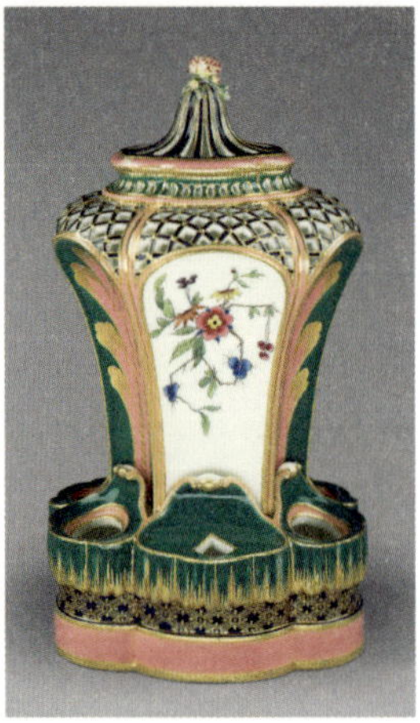

Figs. 7–8
Painted decoration attributed to Charles-Nicolas Dodin, manufactured by Sèvres Manufactory, *Vase (pot-pourri fontaine ou à dauphin)* (obverse and reverse), 1760. Soft-paste porcelain; bleu lapis, blue, pink, and green ground colors, polychrome enamel decoration, and gilding, 29.8 × 16.5 × 14.6 cm. J. Paul Getty Museum, Los Angeles, 78.DE.358.2.

of the colors practically unique to soft-paste porcelain. It was first introduced around 1756–57 but does not appear in the records of the Sèvres manufactory until 1758, when its inventor, Philippe Xhrowet, was paid for his innovation.[36]

Porcelain wares with bodies in *rose* (French for pink) were reissued by Sèvres every few years in the 1760s. Items were generally released in new colors around Christmas as a way of capitalizing on novelty. Pompadour purchased Sèvres porcelain in all colors, but some of her most spectacular pieces were pink, as were some of the most impressive pieces belonging to Louis XV. Pink of a lighter, rich rose—untinged by purple—was seen as characteristic of Sèvres, because it could not be replicated on the hard-paste porcelain produced by rival manufactory Meissen. Most recognizable today as exemplary of Pompadour's tastes are works with Chinese-style figures painted by the great Sèvres illustrator Charles-Nicolas Dodin over the manufactory's famous ground color *fond rose*.[37] Dodin decorated his reserves with images of women going about everyday life: educating children, for instance, or undertaking genteel feminine pursuits in the confines of the home. The sources of the figures have not been positively identified; while scholars have suggested that they might come from Chinese porcelain or enamels, the fact that no clear predecessor has been identified lays open the possibility that they were the express creations of Dodin.[38] The imaginative aspects of the figures seem especially heightened on the pieces he created for Pompadour, the majority of which were made in the last few years of her life

36. Rosalind Savill, *The Wallace Collection Catalogue of Sèvres Porcelain*, vol. 3 (London: Wallace Collection, 1988), 1175.

37. For these as *fond rose*, see Bailey, "Madame de Pompadour," 229. Authors such as Svend Eriksen have noted that Pompadour's full inventory of porcelain included more blue pieces than pink by a fair number. See Svend Eriksen, *Sèvres Porcelain*, James A. de Rothschild Collection at Waddesdon Manor 2 (Fribourg, Switzerland: Office du Livre, 1968), 31. Marie-Laure de Rochebrune likewise posits that Pompadour's devotion to pink is played up in relation to the total number of pieces of that color owned by the marquise. See Marie-Laure de Rochebrune, "La passion de madame de Pompadour pour la porcelaine," in Salmon, *Madame de Pompadour et les Arts*, 411. Of the surviving pieces known to have been owned by Pompadour, however, many of the most spectacular feature a pink ground.

38. On the lack of identified sources, see Marie-Laure de Rochebrune, *Splendeur de la peinture sur porcelaine au XVIIIe siècle: Charles Nicolas Dodin et la manufacture de Vincennes-Sèvres* (Paris: Editions Arlys, 2012), 79.

(1760–63). The women are ciphers for Pompadour herself, and the pink bodies of the ceramics are intimately linked with the themes of femininity and maternity. On a *pot-pourri fontaine* in the J. Paul Getty Museum, for instance, a child learns to walk with the help of two women, one of whom bends down to steady him (Fig. 7). In all cases, the women are removed from the larger (masculine) world. Each of Dodin's works depicts in the reserve on the side opposite the Chinese figures a detailed painting of flowers against a brilliant white background (Fig. 8).

Flowers lend their names to the word for a mixture of red and white in both English (pink) and French (rose). As is perhaps appropriate for the namesake of a plant that bursts forth before withering away, pink has been associated throughout the history of Western European art with blood and fertility. The Christ Child was often depicted in Renaissance art reaching out to pluck a pink carnation from the hands of John the Baptist, seen as foretelling his mortal crucifixion. Alternately referred to as a "pink" in English, the carnation—whose name evokes incarnation, or the state of being made of flesh—is thus associated with blood and death. Carnations also frequently appeared in betrothal portraits, perhaps following the flower's link with blood to fertility and birth, the ultimate objective of betrothal. Unlike today, when pink is stereotypically associated with young girls, in the eighteenth century it was often the color of fertility and motherhood.[39] Notably, with her stilled hands and frontal positioning, Pompadour takes on an icon-like pose in the Harvard portrait that evokes images of both the Madonna and the Christ Child in religious Renaissance works (compare, for instance, *The Virgin and Child*

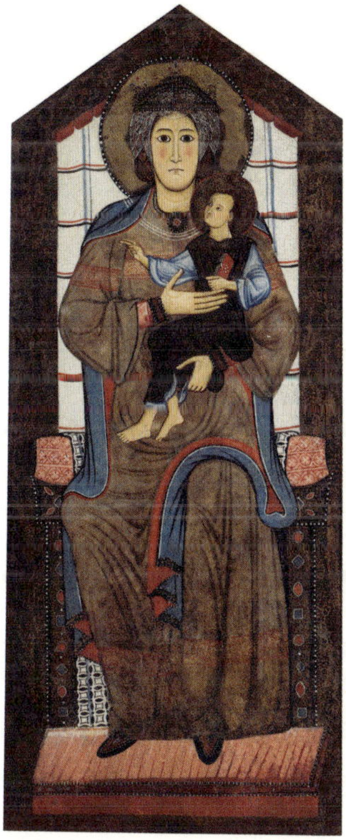

Fig. 9
Master of Camerino, *The Virgin and Child Enthroned*, c. 1270. Tempera and silver on panel, transferred to new support, 108.6 × 47.6 cm. Harvard Art Museums/Fogg Museum, Gift of John Nicholas Brown, 1969.151.

39. For further discussion, see A. Cassandra Albinson, "Feminine Desire and Fragility: Pink in Eighteenth-Century Portraiture," in *Pink: The History of a Punk, Pretty, Powerful Color*, ed. Valerie Steele (New York: Thames and Hudson, 2018).

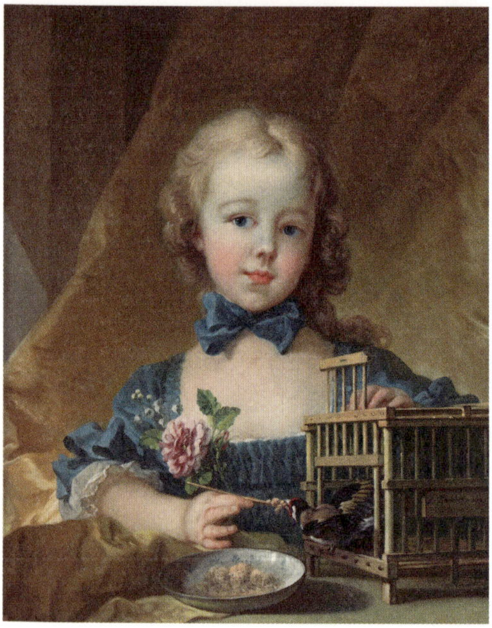

Enthroned by the Master of Camerino; Fig. 9). She is Madonna and child in one.[40]

Pompadour's daughter died years before the Harvard portrait was made (or enlarged, whatever the case), and she is of course missing from representations of the marquise while at court—it would not have been appropriate to include the daughter born of Pompadour's cuckolded husband. Yet a newly discovered portrait of Alexandrine by Boucher, painted in 1749, holds intriguing clues about the nature of pink in the portrait of Pompadour (Fig. 10). Unlike her mother, young Alexandrine is shown all in blue, the color of innocence and the Virgin Mary. This tradition grew out of works such as *The Crucifixion* by Ambrogio Lorenzetti, now in the Harvard Art Museums, where we see the Virgin in her blue robe collapsed with grief and Mary Magdalene swathed in red standing near her (Fig. 11). In the portrait of Alexandrine, the girl's arm and hand placement is uncannily similar to that of her mother in the Harvard painting; instead of applying rouge, however, the child releases a bird from its cage to feed it, indicative of a nurturing spirit. Her pale skin contrasts with her mother's rouged cheeks, but the portraits have much in common, including their frontal-facing posture and almost identical bows at the neck. The key difference lies in the color: pink versus blue, mature versus innocent. Yet this opposition binds the figures together.

Fig. 10
François Boucher, *Alexandrine Le Normant d'Etiolles*, 1749. Oil on canvas, 54.5 × 46 cm. Château de Versailles, V.2019.29.

40. For this association, I thank Ewa Lajer-Burcharth and the Harvard graduate students in the Spring 2020 course Works of Art: Materials, Forms, Histories.

Pompadour owned a miniature after the painting of her daughter roughly the size of the carved gem of Louis XV that she wears

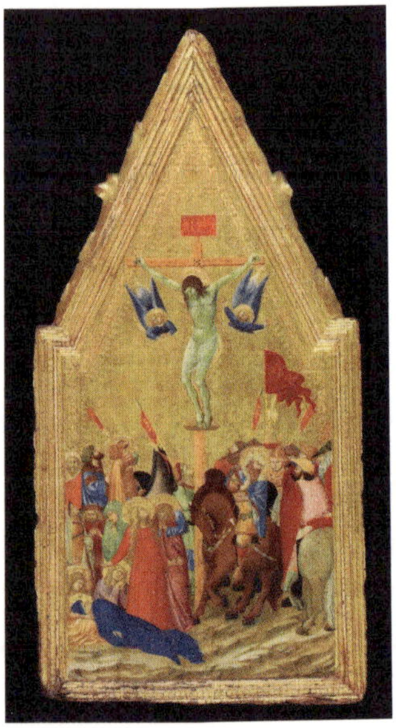

Fig. 11
Ambrogio Lorenzetti, *The Crucifixion*, c. 1345. Tempera and gold leaf on panel with engaged frame, 61 × 29 cm. Harvard Art Museums/Fogg Museum, Gift of Paul J. Sachs in honor of Edward W. Forbes's thirtieth year as director of the Fogg Museum, 1939.113.

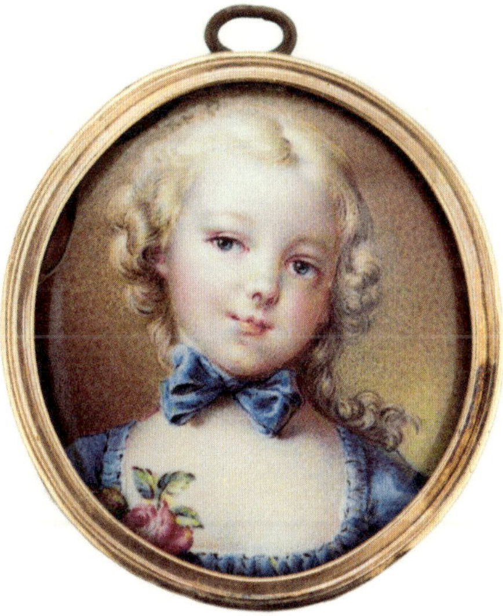

Fig. 12
Louis François Marie Aubert, after François Boucher, *Alexandrine Le Normant d'Etiolles,* c. 1751. Ivory miniature with copper frame, 3 × 2.6 cm. Musée Lambinet, Versailles, 596.

on her wrist in the Harvard portrait (Fig. 12). The miniature hovers over the portrait of Pompadour, a hidden representation of the loving, maternal sensibility less obvious than the amorous love stressed in the painting of the marquise. The daughters of eighteenth-century women pictured at their toilettes were often included in such portraits, as a means of suggesting that the mother passed on beauty and grooming rituals to her daughter, preparing her for a life of successful marriage and intimacy. Images such as Nattier's portrait of Madame Marsollier and her daughter, shown at the Salon of 1750 (Fig. 13), and a family portrait by François-Hubert Drouais now in the National Gallery of Art in Washington, D.C. (Fig. 14) would have been familiar to Pompadour; they make the absence of her child in the Harvard portrait all the more poignant.[41] In both paintings, the mother is about to place a blue flower in the child's hair. Scholars have surmised that before the Harvard portrait was altered to depict Pompadour applying rouge, she held in her hand not a brush but

41. Chrisman-Campbell, "Dressing to Impress," 67.

Fig. 13
Jean-Marc Nattier, *Madame Marsollier and Her Daughter*, 1749. Oil on canvas, 146.1 × 114.3 cm. Metropolitan Museum of Art, New York, Bequest of Florence S. Schuette, 45.172.

Fig. 14
François-Hubert Drouais, *Family Portrait*, 1756. Oil on canvas, 244 × 195 cm. National Gallery of Art, Washington, D.C., Samuel H. Kress Collection, 1946.7.4.

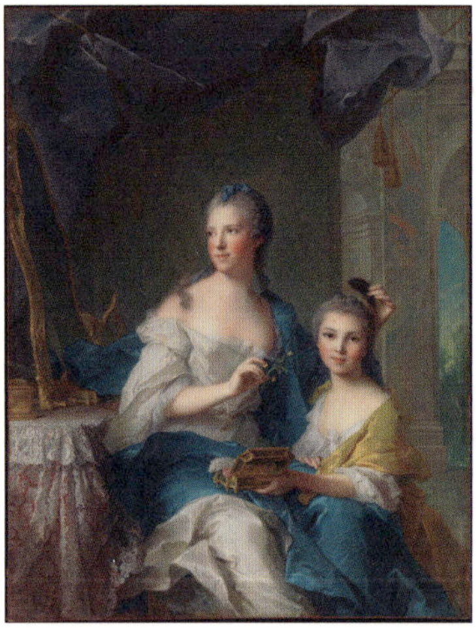

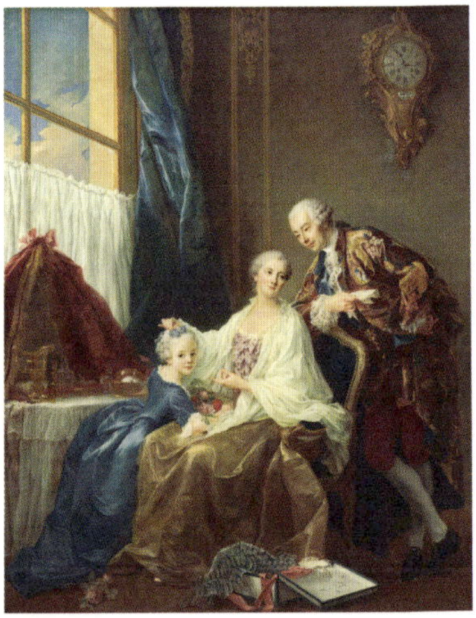

a blue flower, which would have linked the portraits of mother and daughter more concretely.[42] Pompadour's motherhood and fecundity are suggested by the color pink, yet death and loss, as well as her position as mistress to the king, made the manifestation of those qualities—her child—unpicturable.

In Pompadour's lifetime, the norms of parent/child relationships were beginning to undergo drastic change. In 1762, two years before the marquise's death, Jean-Jacques Rousseau published *Émile*, an educational treatise arguing that children should be brought up in close proximity to their parents and taught empathy and sensitivity to others as they mature.[43] The family portrait had also grown in popularity since first appearing in French art around 1700; these works tended to stress not only love for children but love between a husband and wife.[44] The Drouais portrait, an early and novel celebration of the familial

42. Gordon and Hensick, "The Picture within the Picture," 22.

43. In discussing Pompadour's sensibility as expressed in the Harvard portrait and in relation to the portrait of her daughter, we must recognize that her emotional expansiveness did not seem to extend to concern with the wider suffering caused by slavery (or by poverty in France, for that matter). On her family's investment in the slave trade and the two Black serving-people in her retinue, see Oliver Wunsch's essay in this volume. For humanitarianism as a definition of sensibility, see Daniel Wickberg, "What Is the History of Sensibilities? On Cultural Histories, Old and New," *American Historical Review* 112 (3) (June 2007): 679–80.

44. Emma Barker, "'No Picture More Charming': The Family Portrait in Eighteenth-Century France," *Art History* 40 (3): 528.

bonds between an unidentified mother, father, and child, was one of the most famous. Combining family portrait and toilette scene, the painting brings to life the lover and child haunting Boucher's portrait.[45] The juxtaposition underlines the self-determination of Pompadour as portrayed at her dressing table, the aloneness that is tribute to her singularity. This representation of an independent Pompadour fixing herself for the gaze of others, rather than drawing back from it, is surely one of the reasons that the painting has received wide interest and acclaim. There is nothing shy or removed about the marquise in this portrait. Yet the colors with which she is rendered cement her emotional bonds with Louis XV and Alexandrine, thereby linking the painting to larger cultural shifts not normally associated with Madame de Pompadour.

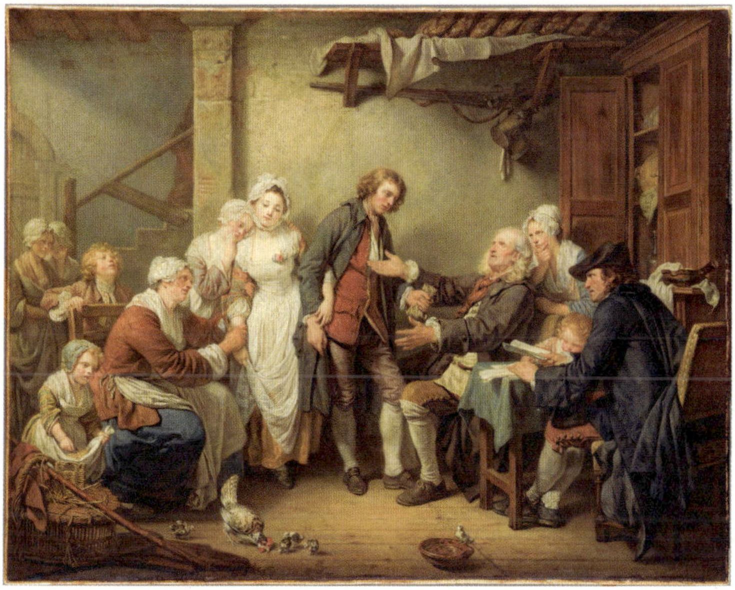

Fig. 15
Jean-Baptiste Greuze, *L'Accordée de village* (The Marriage Contract), 1761. Oil on canvas, 92 × 117 cm. Musée du Louvre, Paris, INV 5037.

The maternal theme featured heavily in the imagery associated with Pompadour in the last years of her life, when mother and child were brought together not by Boucher's brush but by the painters of her pink Sèvres china. This aligns with the broader trend in French art of portraying sentimentalized depictions of family bonding and loving relations between men and women. The year before *Émile* was published, Pompadour's brother commissioned Jean-Baptiste Greuze to paint *L'Accordée de village* (The Marriage Contract; Fig. 15), a painting that caused a sensation upon its exhibition at the Salon of 1761. At its center are the intertwined figures of the betrothed, the bride overtaken by emotion at

45. For more on the Drouais portrait, see Carol Duncan, "Happy Mothers and Other New Ideas in French Art," *The Art Bulletin* 55 (4) (December 1973): 579. Duncan notes that it was created when concepts of familial bliss "were still relatively novel in France."

the thought of her impending marriage. Thomas Crow has noted that the left side of the painting, peopled mostly by female figures, "is dominated by the broad note of white in the bride's dress and rhythm of white blended with pink and lavender in the linen of the other women and the child."[46] In other words, the bride and her family are denoted coloristically by pale pinks and lavenders. Certainly, Pompadour was a great consumer of luxury goods and an active artist in her own right. The pinks in the Harvard portrait, however, compel us to recognize her role in a cultural moment that saw the valorization of private and loving relationships like those between Pompadour and Louis XV, kept close at her wrist, and between the marquise and her daughter, whose spirit lingers in the dressing room.

46. Thomas E. Crow, *Painters and Public Life in Eighteenth-Century Paris* (New Haven, Conn.: Yale University Press, 1985), 149.

"Many Truths of Nature and a Rich, Flowing Brush"

Boucher, Pink, and the Culture of Natural History

Mark Ledbury

EARLIER ACCOUNTS OF BOUCHER'S portrait of *Pompadour at Her Toilette* emphasize the sitter's involvement in constructing her own image.[1] By refocusing attention on the decision-making, range of knowledge, and artistic practice that its painter, rather than its patron, brought to bear, my aim here is not to refute those insightful readings, but instead to consider the ways in which the painting was shaped by Boucher and his culture. An artist nearly as defamed as his subject, Boucher was a man of constantly fertile pictorial intelligence (to borrow Svetlana Alpers and Michael Baxandall's term[2]) who, 250 years after his death, we can finally understand as one of the universal painters of his century: the most versatile, gifted, and fluent French history painter to work in a mythological mode;[3] an able and inexhaustible designer, decorator, and creator of worlds and genres; and as recent Pompadour literature has

1. Elise Goodman-Soellner, "Boucher's *Madame de Pompadour at Her Toilette*," *Simiolus* 17 (1) (1987): 41–58; Elise Goodman, *The Portraits of Madame de Pompadour: Celebrating the Femme Savante* (Berkeley: University of California Press, 2000); Melissa Hyde, "The 'Makeup' of the Marquise: Boucher's Portrait of Pompadour at Her Toilette," *The Art Bulletin* 82 (3) (2000): 453–75; Ewa Lajer-Burcharth, "Pompadour's Touch: Difference in Representation," *Representations* 73 (1) (2001): 54–88; Alden R. Gordon and Teri Hensick, "The Picture within the Picture: Boucher's 1750 Portrait of Madame de Pompadour Identified," *Apollo* 155 (480) (February 2002): 21–30; Xavier Salmon, *Madame de Pompadour et les Arts* (Paris: Réunion des musées nationaux, 2002), 152–54, no. 30; Ewa Lajer-Burcharth, *The Painter's Touch: Boucher, Chardin, Fragonard* (Princeton, N.J.: Princeton University Press, 2018), esp. chap. 1, 80–88; and Melissa Hyde, "The Makeup of the Marquise," in *Making Up the Rococo: François Boucher and His Critics*, Texts & Documents (Los Angeles: Getty Research Institute, 2006), chap. 3, which acknowledges the continuing uncertainty surrounding the date of the painting and its relationship to the rectangular portrait discussed in the Pompadour/Marigny correspondence (see Cassandra Albinson's essay in this volume). See also Melissa Hyde, "Getting into the Picture: Boucher's Self-Portraits of Others," in *Rethinking Boucher*, ed. Melissa Hyde and Mark Ledbury (Los Angeles: Getty Publications, 2006), 13–38.

2. Svetlana Alpers and Michael Baxandall, *Tiepolo and the Pictorial Intelligence* (New Haven, Conn.: Yale University Press, 1996).

shown, a painter who demonstrated an astonishingly consistent quality and conceptual clarity as a portraitist.

What has held us back from fully embracing such a view is a now familiar but nevertheless pernicious and long-lived counter-narrative ingrained in modern art criticism since Diderot.[4] Arsène Houssaye's typically negative account of Boucher in an 1843 article spuriously accused the artist of saying "he found nature extremely disagreeable, too green and badly lit."[5] Purportedly from a letter to fellow painter Nicolas Lancret, this quote has neither been confirmed nor reliably sourced by subsequent scholarship, yet it lives on, irresistible and ubiquitous.

In this essay, I argue against this accusation by focusing on the close and thoughtful attention Boucher paid to the natural world—its colors, forms, and variety—in creating the Pompadour portrait. If we view the work with eyes alert to a rich imagination that saw nature as being in harmony with the confected world, the painting becomes a portal into the surprisingly capacious areas of Boucher's knowledge and intelligence—qualities that a new generation of scholars is beginning to uncover.[6]

3. One need only study Boucher's engagement with Ovid to reach this conclusion, as has been cogently argued since at least 1992, in Colin B. Bailey et al., *The Loves of the Gods: Mythological Painting from Watteau to David* (New York: Rizzoli; Fort Worth, Tex.: Kimbell Art Museum, 1992), esp. 371–428.

4. For an analysis of these modernist prejudices, see Hyde, *Making Up the Rococo*, chap. 1, 1–28.

5. "[I]l trouva la nature fort désagréable, trop verte, mal éclairée." Arsène Houssaye, "Boucher et la Peinture sous Louis XV," *Revue des Deux Mondes: Recueil de La Politique, de l'administration et Des Moeurs*, July 1843. Houssaye's article was reprinted in the journal *L'Artiste* in 1844 and again in his collected writings *Galerie de portraits par A. H. Le dix-huitième siècle. Les poëtes et les philosophes. La cour et le théâtre. La peinture. Nouvelle édition* (Paris: 1845).

6. See especially Jessica Priebe, "Conchyliologie to Conchyliomanie: The Cabinet of François Boucher, 1703–1770," Ph.D. diss., University of Sydney, 2011. Priebe's dissertation has inspired other investigations that make clear the extent of Boucher's passion for the natural world, forthcoming as *François Boucher and the Luxury of Art in Paris, 1703–1770: Artist, Collector, and Connoisseur* (Taylor & Francis). See also Jessica Priebe, "The Artist as Collector: François Boucher (1703–1770)," *Journal of the History of Collections* 28 (1) (2016): 27–42. The present essay is indebted to Priebe's work on many levels. See also Bettina Dietz and Thomas Nutz, "Collections Curieuses: The Aesthetics of Curiosity and Elite Lifestyle in Eighteenth-Century Paris," *Eighteenth-Century Life* 29 (3) (2005): 44–75, which discusses Boucher among other collectors; and Bettina Dietz, "Mobile Objects: The Space of Shells in Eighteenth-Century France," *British Journal for the History of Science* 39 (3) (2006): 363–82.

From Garden to Cabinet

To pursue my line of inquiry, I consider the shapes, colors, and ordonnance of the Harvard painting, as well as the specific choices Boucher made in both its original design (see Fig. 1) and the incarnation visible today. If there is a key to any narrative discernible in the "picture within the picture," as Alden Gordon and Teri Hensick dubbed the initial iteration, it is in Boucher's use of flowers, color, and texture.[7] The striking pink of Pompadour's bows, the colors of her transparent dressing gown (pearly white tinged with green), the flowers in her hair, the pearled surface of the upholstery, and the pearls she wears as jewelry are all present in the earlier design. What's more, it seems the marquise was once depicted in the act of choosing a flower, most likely to adorn a hair clip or fastener—a beautifying rite that suggests the composition already contained a proto-toilette scene. Beyond securing her elaborate braids in place, the floral hairpiece would serve to complement the rich silks and lace of her outfit. Thus, it can be said that the concept of the Harvard portrait's initial design—so far as we can deduce from an X-ray—revolved around the pairing of complementary or matching colors and forms from the natural world with those that are artificial.

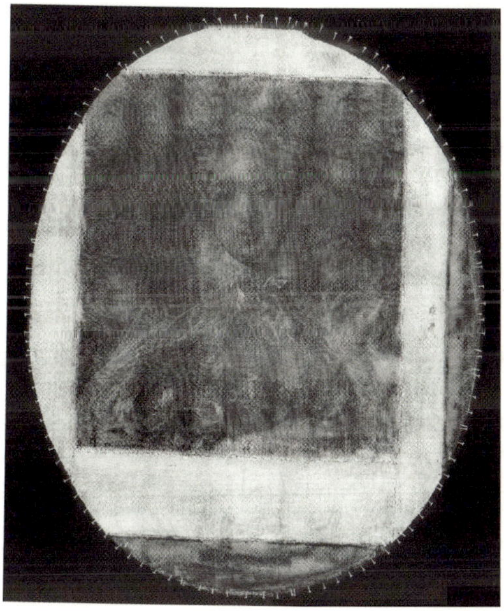

Fig. 1
X-radiograph of *Pompadour at Her Toilette*. Straus Center for Conservation and Technical Studies, Harvard Art Museums, Alan Burroughs Collection of X-Radiographs, 1966.47.

Flower-picking is more conspicuous in Carle Vanloo's portrait of the marquise as a gardener (Fig. 2), but the tone of his (we suspect later) painting deviates from Boucher's intimate, indoor scene. Vanloo's color scheme, for one, highlights Pompadour's features in unflattering ways: her

7. Gordon and Hensick, "The Picture within the Picture."

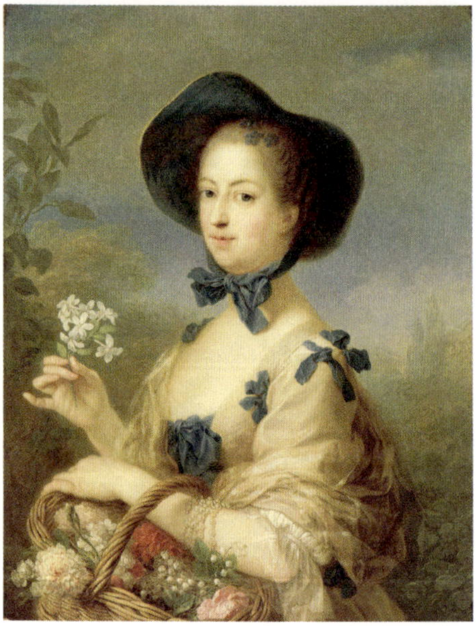

Fig. 2
Carle Vanloo, *Jeanne-Antoinette Poisson, Marquise de Pompadour, en "belle jardinière"* (Jeanne-Antoinette Poisson, Marquise de Pompadour, as Gardener), 1754–55. Oil on canvas, 81.2 × 64.8 cm. Château de Versailles, MV 8616.

deep blue hat and ribbons darken her eyes, the brim casts a shadow over her face, and the white jasmine in her hand evokes (perhaps unintentionally) a slanderous epigram by Jean-Frédéric Phélypeaux, Count of Maurepas, that likely cost the count his position.[8] Boucher opted for a very different palette. In the Harvard portrait, touches of pink and blue play off each other harmoniously, and the contrast between Pompadour's full, alabaster face, powdered hair, and the blue-violet flowers tucked in her braids sets off and accentuates the shape and color of her eyes. Perhaps the sitter herself recognized this refinement when she declared (according to one theory) that the portrait was good but not a likeness.[9] It is tempting to interpret the final choice of gentian violets for the hair as a nod to the flower's various symbolic associations, which included messages of love (it was emblematic of Aphrodite) but also constancy and subtlety, as compared to the rose in poetry of the time.[10] We might infer from the surface visible today that, in the original design, Pompadour was in the midst of a symbolically freighted decision. Without knowing the color of the overpainted flower in her hand, our further interpretation in this vein is limited; but given Boucher's gift for depicting flowers, artifacts, and jewels worn in the hair, it is reasonable to conclude that neither patron nor portrait convention alone guided this early choice. Rather, the artist was intentionally bringing nature indoors, transferring the garden into the cabinet.

Whatever transformations to the image were effected by Boucher between its putative creation in 1750 and its

8. On the portrait, see Salmon, *Madame de Pompadour et les Arts*, 158–60, cat. 34. On the epigram, which made a cruel allusion to "white flowers" in reference to the marquise's salaciously reported vaginal discharge, see André Picciola, "L'activité littéraire du comte de Maurepas," *Dix-Huitième Siècle* 3 (1) (1971): 281; and André Picciola, *Le Comte de Maurepas: Versailles et l'Europe à la fin de l'Ancien Régime* (Paris: Perrin, 1999).

9. See the letter from April 23, 1750, in *Correspondance de Mme. de Pompadour avec son père, m. Poisson, et son frère, m. de Vandières* (Paris: J. Baur, 1878), 50, letter 9.

10. See, for example, Charles-François Panard, *Conseils donnés à une jeune demoiselle pour le jour de sa fête* (Paris: 1753), 8: "La rose orgueilleuse & superbe / Recherche l'éclat du grand jour / L'humble violette sous l'herbe / Fixe son modeste séjour / Celle-ci long-tems est fleurie / L'autre ne dure qu'un soleil / Laquelle des deux, je vous prie, / Prendrez-vous pour votre conseil?" (The rose, splendid and proud, seeks the glare of bright sunlight; while the violet, humble and demure, makes her home discreetly among the grasses. The violet's bloom endures; the rose bloom lasts but a day; which of these, I ask, should you admire and emulate?)

possible remaking between 1756 and 1759,[11] they were conscious, willed choices made by an artist at the peak of his creative powers. If we take as correct the chronology outlined by Gordon, the reworking of the Harvard portrait followed swiftly on the heels of Boucher's 1756 painting of Pompadour reclining in private quarters (see p. 33), one of the most stunning, confident portraits of the century, now in the Alte Pinakothek in Munich. Colin Bailey has argued that the sketches at Waddesdon Manor and in the Wallace Collection in London were likely preliminary ideas for the portrait, made in or around 1756.[12] A painting by Boucher of Pompadour outdoors now in the Victoria and Albert Museum is, like the Harvard canvas, signed and dated 1758. We can therefore say with some certainty that in the years 1756 to 1759, Boucher spent considerable time and effort contemplating and creating a variety of elaborate images of the marquise both in and out of doors.

If the idea behind the original image was to bring nature into the cabinet, to cultivate a modest garden in the toilette, the more fully articulated surfaces of the painting's current state direct us to yet more points of entry rooted in the world of natural history. In the extant version, nature and beautifully human-crafted objects of all kinds are on display. No longer in the act of selecting a flower, Pompadour has chosen the violets in her hair over the pink and yellow flowers presented to her as options, and the pink ribbons finishing her ensemble over the blue ribbon discarded on the dressing table. Boucher, too, has enacted a series of choices in depicting these items and others festooning Pompadour and her toilette—deliberate choices that reveal his penchant for the forms and colors of nature.

11. Gordon and Hensick, "The Picture within the Picture"; and Alden Gordon, "Public and Private in the Art Patronage of the Marquise de Pompadour," Paul Raether Lecture, Trinity College, Hartford, Conn., October 20, 2011; available at https://www.youtube.com/watch?v=Qk8anKNGN64. See also Albinson's essay in this volume.

12. Colin B. Bailey, "Madame de Pompadour. London," *The Burlington Magazine* 145 (1200) (2003): 230–31.

Boucher and the Culture of the Shell

Let us turn first to the pink ribbons to ask: What valences did this color have in the mid-eighteenth century? And how did Boucher arrive at his subtle and varied use of it? While Venetian color and other painterly precedents perhaps inspired him, pink was not dominant in the work of any of Boucher's masters or closest peers. In fact, he deployed the color as part of a broader, long-term endeavor to develop a distinctive palette and brushwork that would mark him out from François Lemoyne, the Coypels, and any others he might have seen as rivals.[13] Recent scholarship and exhibitions have connected pink's reputation for decorative irreality and its utility to fashion with the relative scarcity of the hue in nature.[14] On the contrary, I argue that Boucher's inspiration for the variety of pinks in his oeuvre came directly from nature. Although the pinks of floral culture are actively figured in the Harvard painting, a more fertile starting point for investigating Boucher's preferred shades is the world of conchology, a branch of natural history devoted to the collection, classification, and display of seashells, particularly those belonging to mollusks.

In the mid-eighteenth century, conchology was an aesthetic pursuit through which Boucher and his contemporaries would have come to know and admire different shades of pink. Shell collecting vastly expanded the repertoire of pinkness, so to speak, as colonial trading made new specimens available and scientific publications described their properties. Although the subtle variations of pink found in the collections of shells built up by Boucher and his fellow aficionados have faded over time, contemporary accounts of seashells of various types surpass even discussions of botany in their use of *rose* or *couleur de rose* as descriptors. This is particularly true of the groundbreaking *L'histoire naturelle*

13. See Alastair Laing, "Boucher ou l'invention d'un langage," in *François Boucher, 1703–1770* (New York: Metropolitan Museum of Art, 1986), 62–63.

14. Valerie Steele, ed., *Pink: The History of a Punk, Pretty, Powerful Color* (New York: Thames and Hudson, 2018).

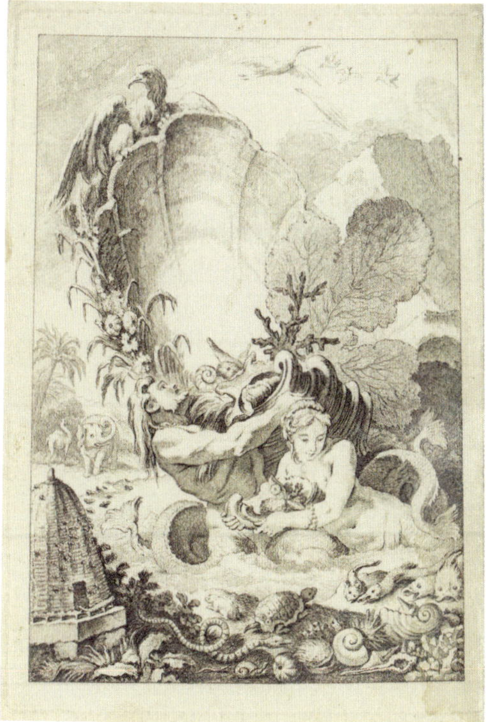

Fig. 3
Frontispiece designed by François Boucher for Dézallier d'Argenville's *La Conchyliologie*, 1757. Engraving, plate: 25.4 × 17.8 cm; sheet: 26.3 × 18.2 cm. Victoria and Albert Museum, London, E.509-1991.

éclaircie dans deux de ses parties principales, la lithologie et la conchyliologie [...], one of the first systematic and scientifically inspired accounts of shells and the creatures that occupy them. First published by connoisseur, aesthete, garden expert, and collector Antoine-Joseph Dézallier d'Argenville in 1742, the work became an authoritative guide for collectors and *curieux*.[15] It was revised and republished in 1757, with a frontispiece designed by Boucher (Fig. 3).[16] In a posthumous edition published in 1780, the word *rose* is mentioned more than two hundred times, either by itself or in the phrase *couleur de rose*.[17] One extract among many from that edition points to the loving and detailed descriptions of color that inform the volume and highlight the importance of pink in classification:

> The "Fly-Bite" Lepas [barnacle]...is decorated with radiating flutes, irregularly marked with pink or cerise spots, on a white surface. Its base is lightly serrated; the summit opening is bordered with pink. Inside, this limpet is off-white, mixed with a little reddish color, and transparent green. The summit hole seems almost round, and the protrusion

15. Antoine-Joseph Dézallier d'Argenville, *L'histoire naturelle éclaircie dans deux de ses parties principales, la lithologie et la conchyliologie: Dont l'une traite des pierres et l'autre des coquillages: Ouvrage dans lequel on trouve une nouvelle méthode & une notice critique des principaux auteurs qui ont écrit sur ces matiéres: Enrichi de figures dessinées d'après nature* (Paris: Chez de Bure l'aîné, 1742).

16. Antoine-Joseph Dézallier d'Argenville, *L'histoire naturelle éclaircie dans une de ses parties principales, la conchyliologie, qui traite des coquillages de mer, de rivière et de terre: ouvrage dans lequel on trouve une nouvelle méthode latine & françoise de les diviser; augmentée de la zoomorphose, ou représentation des animaux à coquilles, avec leurs explications* (Paris: Chez de Bure l'aîné, 1757); hereafter simply *Conchyliologie* 1757. For extensive analysis of this text and Boucher's frontispiece in the literature on the artist, see Priebe, "Conchyliologie to Conchyliomanie."

17. Antoine-Joseph Dézallier d'Argenville, *La conchyliologie, ou histoire naturelle des coquilles de mer, d'eau douce, terrestres et fossiles, avec un traité de la zoomorphose, ou représentation des animaux qui les habitent*, vol. 2 (Paris: Chez de Bure l'aîné, 1780).

surrounding it is of a white color tinged with a green hue, with a pink border.[18]

Varieties of pink are also described in myriad descriptions of collections in auction sales catalogues, such as one for the Verdier sale in 1756.[19] Boucher was known to frequent these auctions as he built up his own impressive collection, about which one contemporary visitor wrote: "This disciple of Albani, whose brush, guided by the graces, offers us only gay and laughing images, owns a curious cabinet, which gives as much pleasure as instruction. The ingenious painter has placed his shells on tables covered with mirrors; to the viewer, they have the aspect of a spectacular floral design in a delicately and carefully crafted parterre that mimics in miniature the garden of nature."[20]

Attentive as it was to fine distinctions of pink, and indeed to color variants in general, conchology surely informed Boucher's repeated and nuanced use of what might be called "shell pink" hues, which he employed in brilliant counterpoint to both pastel blues and more pronounced violets across his oeuvre. Pink is certainly a defining color of the Harvard portrait, and Boucher employs it discerningly: the pink of the bodice ribbons is, as far as we now can tell—varnish and fading notwithstanding—differentiated lovingly through shadows and highlights; it contrasts with the slightly lighter pinks that describe the flower on the dressing table and in subtler (but still conspicuous) ways with the stunning pink of the engraved bracelet clasp (see pp. 6–11). These hues are both centers of attention in the painting and areas of difference and demarcation.

The use of pink for the bracelet clasp in particular represents a deliberate choice on the part of Boucher. As Cassandra Albinson explains in this

18. "*La Piqure de Mouches*... est un Lépas...dorée de cannelures rayonnantes, mouchetées ou piquetées très irrégulièrement de couleur de rose ou de cerise foncé sur un fond blanc. Sa base est légèrement dentelée: le trou du sommet est encore d'un liséré rose; en dedans ce Lépas est blanchâtre mêlé d'un peu de Roussatre, & de vert clair: le trou du sommet y paroit presque rond, & la saillie qui l'entoure est d'un blanc teint de verdâtre, bordé de couleur de rose." Antoine-Joseph Dézallier d'Argenville and Jacques de Favanne, in ibid., 534; translation mine.

19. *Catalogue des curiosités naturelles du sieur Verdier* (Paris: Jorry and Duschesne, 1756). The catalogue contains over thirty references to different shades of pink.

20. "Cet émule d'Albane, dont le pinceau guidé par les Grâces n'offre que des images riantes, possède un cabinet curieux, aussi agréable qu' instructif. Ce peintre Ingénieux a placé ses coquilles sur des tables couvertes de glaces; elles présentent aux yeux du spectateur un parterre émaillé qui semble le disputer à la nature." A.-R. Liesville, *Noms des collectionneurs d'histoire naturelle en 1767* (1867), 6–7; translation mine.

volume, the representation of Louis XV was likely based on a delicate, multi-hued cameo clasp carved from a sardonyx stone by Jacques Guay (see p. 35), but the object in the painting has been completely transformed. The surface beauty and many hues of Guay's cameo, the highly polished sardonyx and subtle mineral veins he skillfully exploited to highlight the laurel crown on the king's head, are entirely absent in Boucher's depiction; the painter recast the clasp so that the carved, pearly white portrait emerges from a pronounced pink background. Given the artist's brilliance at rendering real-life objects (as demonstrated in the Munich portrait and elsewhere), this change is profound and by no means accidental. Could it be that Boucher, the natural historian and shell connoisseur, reimagined the sardonyx gem cameo as a shell cameo? One contemporary use of newly discovered and documented shells (such as *Lobatus gigas*, the queen conch, first described by Linnaeus in 1758) was as an alternative to gem cameos. Guay's clasp also loses its gold, diamond, and emerald mounting in Boucher's depiction, though the unique shape and fastening structure of the actual piece is carefully delineated. The change might therefore owe as much to Boucher's predilections and knowledge as to Pompadour's own interventions as a (self-) image-maker and even gem engraver.[21] Certainly, the new sobriety of the cameo, its lack of sparkle and shine, acts to emphasize animal and vegetable over mineral, in that Boucher retained Guay's laurel frame and added Pompadour's pearls, which are rhymed in the pinheads on the back of her upholstered chair and are themselves, it seems obvious to point out, the product of shells and sea life.

21. For two stimulating discussions of the possible motivations for and meanings of the differences between the Guay clasp cameo and the painted image, see Hyde, "The 'Makeup' of the Marquise," 469; and Lajer-Burcharth, "Pompadour's Touch," 77. The most exhaustive source on the history of Guay as a gem engraver and his relationship with Pompadour remains Jean François Leturcq, *Notice sur Jacques Guay, graveur sur pierres fines du roi Louis XV* (Paris: Baur, 1873).

Melting Mirrors and the Flow of Form

Shell cameos are often considered less prestigious than gem cameos,[22] and it is conceivable that the precious carved sardonyx and diamonds of Guay's cameo were omitted precisely for this reason: a concession, on Pompadour's part, to the forces of anti-luxury patriotism at a time of war and want. The same could be theorized of the mirror, silver in the original design yet varnished with vernis Martin or shellac in the final painting.[23] However, this transformation might likewise be a sly attempt to substitute mineral with organic matter. Lacquer, in its original form, is also an animal product. Shellac is made from the secretions of the female lac bug, *Kerria lacca*. These exotic animal origins were well known to eighteenth-century craftsmen and artisans, and the fondness that Madame de Pompadour and her circle had for lacquer work has been documented.[24] To know whether the mirror is varnished with lacquer or vernis Martin, an artificial substitute perfected by the Martin family of lacquerware artists (among others), is perhaps too much to ask of this painting, but one could argue that for Boucher—a man whose business was representation—the human imitation of organic material could be celebrated just as readily as the real thing.

As such, I see the transformation of the mirror from silver to lacquer as a symbolic melting of the mineral into an organic surface, a practice that is actually fairly common in the artist's oeuvre. As early as his "solo show" at the residence of collector François Derbais (1732–34), Boucher exhibited paintings in which chariots, quivers, swords, and even rocks melt into a vortex of animal, human, and floral form—their solid state liquefied, evaporated, or bent by the powerful unseen forces of nature and Olympus, marshaled by the painter and his distinct brushwork. It is often remarked that Boucher preferred to depict women

22. James David Draper, "Cameo Appearances," *Metropolitan Museum of Art Bulletin* 65 (4) (2008): 52.

23. See Gordon and Hensick, "The Picture within the Picture," 25–26, Figs. 9–11.

24. Gerald Reitlinger, *The Economics of Taste*, vol. 2 (London: Barrie & Rockliff, 1963).

as if "without bones."[25] If we see this as evidence not of a lack of anatomical skills but instead of his predilection for the *flow of form*, for the sea snails and other boneless marvels described in the sections of *Conchyliologie* devoted to animals in 1757, we can consider anew the fluidity that is frequently at the heart of Boucher's work. Astute commentators both past and present have recognized this skill, including the great collector and connoisseur Claude-Henri Watelet, who, in a rebuke of painter Julien de Parme, wrote of Boucher's work: "There were many truths of nature and a rich, flowing [*moëlleux*] brush."[26] *Moëlleux*, notably, comes from the French word for marrow, that interior proto-form that nourishes life, a vital creative and healing force, the origin of the flow of cells and blood through the human body.

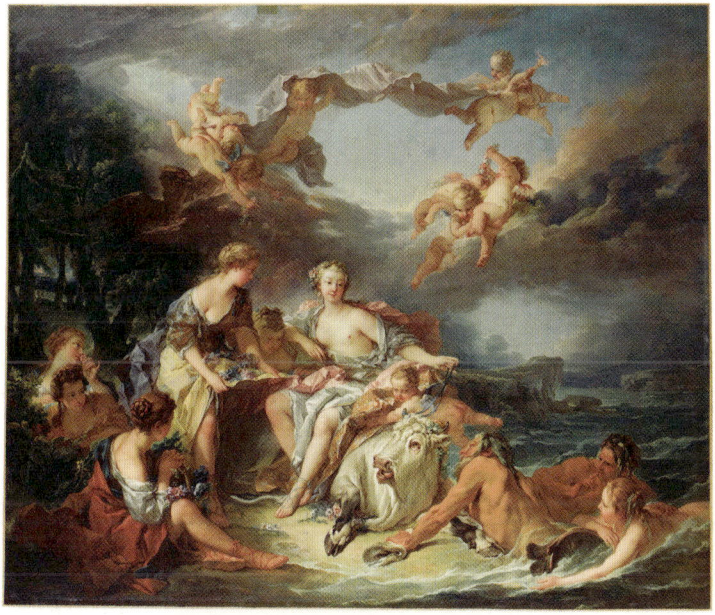

Fig. 4
François Boucher, *Rape of Europa*, 1747. Oil on canvas, 160.5 × 193.5 cm. Musée du Louvre, Paris, Collection de Louis XV, roi de France (1715–1774), acquis en 1747, Département des Peintures, INV 2714.

Examples of such flowing metamorphoses of form can also be seen in the melting rocks of the great Ovidian painting of the century, Boucher's second *Rape of Europa*, submitted to the history painting competition at the Académie royale de peinture et de sculpture in 1747 (Fig. 4). The work also points to another of Boucher's most beguiling and enduring gifts: his ability to rhyme and enmesh human and divine bodies with flora, fauna, and geological forms, employed here for specific and brilliant narrative purpose. The rhyming of flowers, shells, the bull's hoof, and Europa's beribboned foot in the murky liminal space between land and sea is, along with the glassy eye and salivating tongue of

25. See Colin B. Bailey in Bailey et al., *The Loves of the Gods*, 384–85.

26. "[I]l y avait beaucoup de vérités de nature et un pinceau moëlleux." See Pierre Rosenberg, "Une correspondance de Julien de Parme," *Archives de l'Art Français* 26 (1984): 224.

the bull (Jupiter disguised in animal form), part of what makes the painting such a successful and perceptive reading of Ovid's oddly tragicomic tale. But the story's mixture of eroticism and elegance is conjured by Boucher's detailed attention to nature and the human form.

Even the grandest and least realistic Boucher fantasies contain extraordinary moments of naturalistic detail. In the delicate pastoral *The Love Letter*, now in the National Gallery of Art (Fig. 5), the gorgeous and subtle rendering of the shades and ripples of the improbable pink silk gown of one of the pictured confidantes may distract us from the highly naturalistic representation of the droopy-eared dog (feebly imitated in every extant studio or later copy of the painting); the moss-covered barks of the bridge guard or fence (evidence of Boucher's talent for depicting cut wood improvised into barriers); the meticulous detail and execution of the stems and flowers at the feet of the figure in pink; and the harmonious deployment of blue-violet and pink in the floral decor, basket, and dresses—the same scheme at work in the Harvard portrait. A viewer might also miss the surprising details of the bare feet of the lady in pink, whose exaggerated gap between big toe and elongated second digit evokes the cloven hooves all around her.

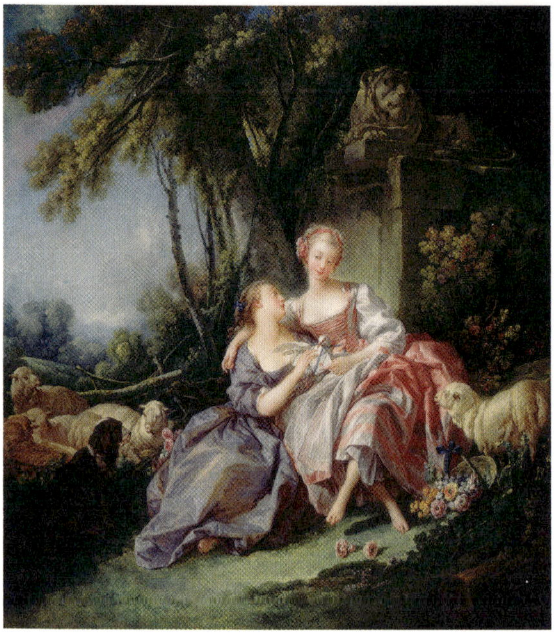

Fig. 5
François Boucher, *The Love Letter*, 1750. Oil on canvas, 81.2 × 75.2 cm. National Gallery of Art, Washington, D.C., Timken Collection, 1960.6.3.

More immediately preceding (or perhaps contemporaneous with) the reworking of the Harvard portrait is Boucher's 1758 painting of Madame de Pompadour reading outdoors (Fig. 6). In this ambitious (and itself much copied) variant of the Munich portrait, Pompadour's braids escape their pins and rhyme with the braided bow around her neck. The combination of the mellow but earthy brown tint and dusky hues of pink in her dress nods to the subtle mix of green, brown, pink, and blue that describes her *locus amoenus*, whose very forms embrace and envelop her drapery, similar to the shell-like spaces of pastoral glades that enfold, for example, the head of Diana in Boucher's 1742 depiction of the goddess at her bath. The Pompadour painting evokes a Theocritean mood; the marquise, distracted by a singing bird, looks up and away from the page that she gently holds between her fingers. The well-thumbed, unbound set of volumes on which she rests her true left arm has rightly inspired scholars to interpret this image as a declaration of her refinement, knowledge, and self-assertiveness, rivaling in certain respects the extraordinary 1752–55 pastel by Maurice-Quentin de La Tour (see p. 32).[27] However, this painting doesn't necessarily point to an amalgam of intellectual talents as much as it harmonizes rustic and intellectual life, the wild and the cultivated, nature and human confection, the bound and the unbound. As in the Munich portrait, the delicately placed and lovingly rendered pair of cut roses, here crossed at the edge of a clear stream or pool so faintly described it is almost imperceptible, align with and echo the crossed feet of the marquise and the jeweled buckle of her shoe. The buckle might be seen as a bucolic substitute for, or transposition of, the elaborate clasp and pearl bracelet of other portraits, as

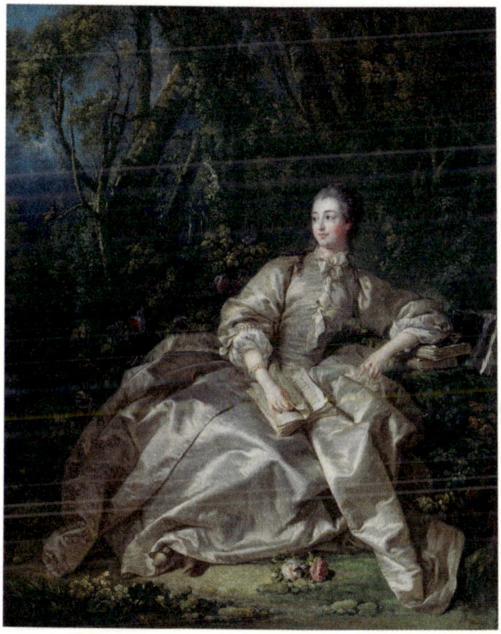

Fig. 6
François Boucher, *Portrait of Madame de Pompadour*, 1758. Oil on canvas, 52.4 × 57.8 cm. Victoria and Albert Museum, London, Bequeathed by John Jones, 487-1882.

27. See especially Goodman, *The Portraits of Madame de Pompadour*. See also Lajer-Burcharth, "Pompadour's Touch."

here the marquise wears only a double string of natural pearls on her wrist. This flowing ensemble demonstrates Boucher's ability to both refine and transfer his pastoral eloquence to a poetic and meditative portrait mode. If we compare this to Vanloo's finely painted but stilted portrait of Pompadour as a gardener (see Fig. 2), whose elegant precision thwarts any sense that the marquise is in her natural habitat, we appreciate Boucher's subtle and suggestive conception all the more.

This evocation of the metamorphosis of human, vegetal, and animal forms may seem far-fetched; consider, however, the notion of *zoomorphose* (zoomorphosis), discussed by Dézallier d'Argenville in his preface and introduction to *Conchyliologie* in 1757 and further elaborated in his correspondence with botanist and fellow collector Antoine de La Faille.[28] In the eighteenth century, *zoomorphose* could refer either to the inhabitation and transformation of vegetal matter by animals (such as creatures that occupy shells) or, more generally, to the zoomorphic conversion of gods or humans into animal form. One could argue that Boucher had a special gift for painterly zoomorphism—for celebrating gods in animal form, yes, but also for giving humans animal qualities and bringing vegetal, animal, and human matter into rhyme and even synthesis.

Returning to the Harvard portrait in this light—imaginatively and primed with an eye toward zoomorphosis—we might find flowers and fountains, shells and mollusks, coral and sponges. These are what I call shadow forms in the painting, like the actual shadow of the flower barely visible above the hand that now holds a makeup brush instead. Does the marquise's dressing gown, with its translucent, aqua-green tint and striking drape (see pp. 4–5), not contain echoes of the flowing waters of Boucher's pastorals? Or of the interiors of seashells, their subtle stripes pearl-white and tinged with green? Improbable as it might be, it is tempting to see depicted in the fabric around her proper right arm the laced exterior and pink interior folds of

28. Antoine-Joseph Dézallier d'Argenville, "Discours Préliminaire sur la Zoomorphose," in *Conchyliologie* 1757, vol. 2, 1–20.

shells. Similarly, the particular brushstrokes and strangely evocative form of the powder applicator (p. 13), with its elegantly shaped handle and spongiform body, simultaneously brings to mind flowers, animal fur, and coral. The decoration on the box that Boucher places in the marquise's other hand, whose pink interior again suggests the lining of a shell, swirls into imprecise form, as do the delicate curls of her ribbons, shaped as a series of cavities distinguished by various shades of pink, and even the oddly multi-colored and almost slithering ribbon on the table (pp. 8–9). It is hard to resist the impression that these human-made trappings of a definitively human activity echo natural forms and structures, from shells and seaworms, to flowers, to corals and sponges.

The final portrait, then, is not only a reflection on making and remaking, or on painting. It is also shaped by the afterimage of a collector's cabinet displayed on a mirrored table: combining spiral, clasping, wondrous natural forms, transmogrified by a bone-marrow brush and an active and clever imagination to become a striking and subtle assertion of a natural as well as a cultural order, of a thoughtful, dedicated, and determined grace. Whether or not we see these ripples beneath the surface of the canvas, spreading out from human self-making to the inspiration of natural wonders, the culture of collecting, and even the anxiety of colonial possession and dispossession, will depend on our willingness to entertain the notion of this painting as part of a complex, always metamorphosing, continuously evolving circuit of forms. This notion is a challenge to our art-historical desire for fixity and precision, perhaps, but the best tribute we can pay to the rich, sinuous, ever-flowing creations of Boucher.

Mark Ledbury is the Power Professor of Art History and Visual Culture and director of the Power Institute at the University of Sydney.

Pompadour, Porcelain, and Pink

Gabriella Szalay

VERY FEW EXTANT PORTRAITS OF MADAME de Pompadour depict objects made of porcelain. A portrait sketch by Boucher from around 1750, now at Waddesdon Manor in Buckinghamshire, England, features a magnificent celadon vase resting on the cabinet at left (Fig. 1). Another, painted by François-Hubert Drouais in 1763 and now in the National Gallery, London, includes a table inlaid with porcelain panels. The otherwise conspicuous lack of porcelain in portraits of the marquise is noteworthy, since, like many members of eighteenth-century European nobility, she was an avid collector of this new and "exotic" material.[1] In keeping with contemporary tastes, she displayed a penchant for Asian and especially Chinese porcelain, although she also collected and commissioned objects from European manufactories such as Meissen, the first to produce "true" or hard-paste porcelain on the continent.[2] According to some modern scholars, Pompadour was even instrumental in the establishment of the French Royal Porcelain Manufactory at Sèvres, which opened its doors in 1756 under the auspices of her lover, Louis XV.[3] So why did relatively few artists who painted her likeness pair it with porcelain?

I want to challenge this artistic tradition by taking a closer look at Harvard's portrait of Madame de Pompadour from

1. Stéphane Castelluccio, *Collecting Chinese and Japanese Porcelain in Pre-Revolutionary Paris*, trans. Sharon Grevet (Los Angeles: J. Paul Getty Museum, 2013), 154.

2. Jean Terrasson, *Madame de Pompadour et la création de la "Porcelaine de France"* (Paris: Bibliothèque des Arts, 1969), 38. According to an inventory conducted after her death in 1764, Pompadour owned 3,187 objects made of porcelain, 221 of which were imported from Asia and 475 of which originated from Meissen. For more on the circumstances that led to the invention of European porcelain in 1708–9, see Martin Schönfeld, "Was There a Western Inventor of Porcelain?" *Technology and Culture* 39 (4) (October 1998): 716–27.

3. The primary proponent of this view is Jean Terrasson. For a strong counterargument, see Antoine d'Albis, "La Marquise de Pompadour et la manufacture de Vincennes," *Sèvres* 1 (1992): 52–63.

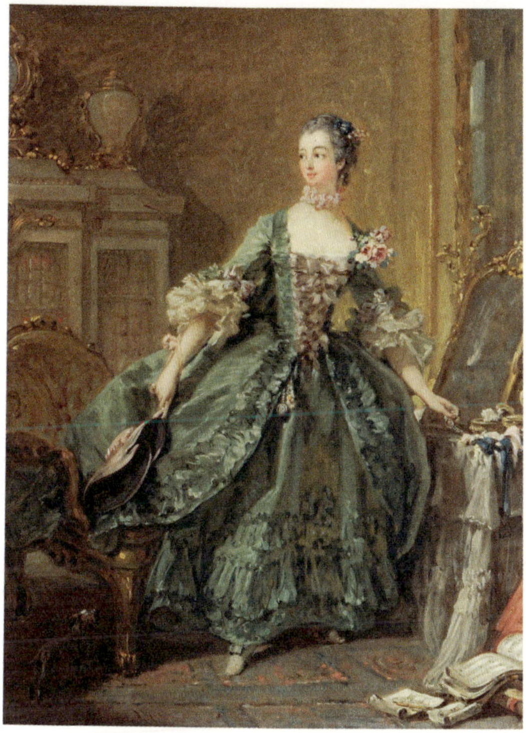

Fig. 1
François Boucher, *Sketch for a Portrait of Madame de Pompadour (1721–1764)*, c. 1750. Oil on canvas, 62.5 × 46 cm. Waddesdon Manor, England, Rothschild Collection, 965.1995.

the point of view of porcelain and color. Dated by some experts to 1750 (with later additions), Boucher's painting features several worldly things that identify the scene as a toilette: a mirror, which Pompadour uses to check her appearance; a gilded silver brush, rouge, and a powder box, all of which enable her to perfect her complexion; and a peignoir, or dressing gown, which protects her other garments from discoloration.[4] While some of these objects have received sustained scholarly attention, the flowers on the dressing table in the foreground have elicited little commentary until this volume. (For a different reading of the flowers, see the essay by Mark Ledbury.) Those who have addressed their presence identify them either as allegorical representations of Pompadour's beauty or as practical adornments for her hair, without stopping to consider other possible meanings.[5] Yet upon careful examination, one could argue that neither their anatomy nor their color corresponds to actual flora. This is especially true of the rose to the right, which assumes a distinct purple hue (see pp. 8–9). Jarring at first glance, the hue is in fact consistent with the appearance of contemporary objects

4. Alden R. Gordon and Teri Hensick, "The Picture within the Picture: Boucher's 1750 Portrait of Madame de Pompadour Identified," *Apollo* 155 (480) (February 2002): 21–30. Combining technical analysis and historical research, Gordon and Hensick surmise that the painting was completed in three phases: the first in 1750, the second from roughly 1759 to 1760, and the third possibly undertaken in the 1760s or 1770s. For readers interested in "thing theory," the classic treatment remains Bill Brown, "Thing Theory," *Critical Inquiry* 28 (1) (Autumn 2001): 1–22.

5. Elise Goodman-Soellner, "Boucher's *Madame de Pompadour at Her Toilette*," *Simiolus* 17 (1) (1987): 45.

made of porcelain, a medium that was (and remains) notoriously difficult to decorate with colors, none more precarious than pink. As I argue, the flowers on Pompadour's dressing table can be read as a subtle commentary on the state of French porcelain in the years before the invention of pink overglaze enamel (*fond rose*) at Sèvres in the later 1750s.[6]

A Rose by Any Other Name

When Boucher began to paint his portrait of Pompadour primping and preening, porcelain flowers were all the rage. Like the material from which they are made, porcelain flowers originated in China, where they were first used as ornamental decoration during the Ming dynasty (1368–1644). The earliest references to Europeans collecting objects decorated in such a manner date from the first half of the eighteenth century, when the luxury dealers, or *marchands merciers*, who helped facilitate the circulation of porcelain from East to West saw an opportunity to expand their trade.[7] Collaborating with local artisans, they crafted elaborate ensembles in which functional objects such as clocks and chandeliers were transformed into spectacular conversation pieces through the addition of precious materials.[8] Porcelain flowers were vital to such ensembles, helping set the stage for attendant allegorical representations and reminding viewers of the contemporary craze for botany and botanizing.

While Pompadour owned numerous ensembles with porcelain flowers from China, she also collected porcelain flowers from the Vincennes manufactory.[9] Founded in 1739–40, when nobleman Jean-Louis-Henri Orry de Fulvy took in two defecting artisans from nearby

6. There are three ways of decorating porcelain: with glazes, which are typically composed of silica and alumina and can be mixed with a colorant, although they are largely translucent; with underglaze enamels, which are composed of metal oxides and are painted onto the ceramic body prior to the application of a glaze; and/or with overglaze enamels, which are likewise composed of metal oxides but are painted onto the ceramic body after it has been glazed.

7. Tamara Préaud, "The Origins and History of Porcelain Flowers," *The French Porcelain Society Journal* 1 (2003): 47. Porcelain was invented in China during the Tang dynasty (618–907).

8. Mimi Hellman, "The Nature of Artifice: French Porcelain Flowers and the Rhetoric of the Garnish," in *The Cultural Aesthetics of Eighteenth-Century Porcelain*, ed. Alden Cavanaugh and Michael E. Yonan (Burlington, Vt.: Ashgate, 2010), 39–64. Hellman notes that between 1745 and 1748, Parisian *marchands merciers* had approximately eighty thousand porcelain flowers in stock.

9. Terrasson, *Madame de Pompadour et la création de la "Porcelaine de France,"* 86–87.

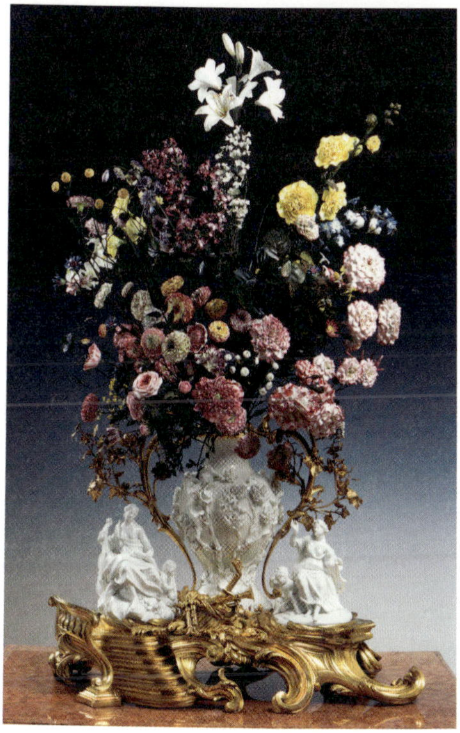

Fig. 2
Jean-Claude Chambellan Duplessis, manufactured by Vincennes Manufactory, *The Porcelain Bouquet*, before 1749. Hard-paste porcelain with polychrome enamel and gold, 115.6 × 65.6 × 43.2 cm. Staatliche Kunstsammlungen Dresden, Porzellansammlung, PE 707.

Chantilly, Vincennes was in many ways typical of other early European porcelain manufactories.[10] Burdened with the task of figuring out how to achieve the same brilliant white ceramic body as Asian potters, its early years were marked by experimentation and financial struggle. By the mid-1740s, however, the manufactory had gained royal support, due in part to its exquisite porcelain flowers.[11] Mounted on stems made of brass wire wrapped in silk, then arranged into artful bouquets housed in vases made of like materials, these flowers became an overnight sensation at French court (Fig. 2). In 1750 alone, Pompadour ordered twenty-four bouquets for her château at Bellevue, each containing dozens or even hundreds of flowers.[12]

Admittedly, the flowers in Boucher's painting do not correspond to such an arrangement. However, it was not unusual to find porcelain flowers displayed as individual blossoms.[13] Their placement on a dressing table, moreover, accords with what we know of artificial flowers writ large in the period; they were frequently found in intimate settings, where they were infused with fragrances intended to mimic the scent of their natural counterparts.[14] While the preferred material for such flowers was silk, porcelain may very well have been used to similar effect,

10. A good overview of the French manufactories that preceded Vincennes can be found in Geneviève Le Duc, *Porcelain tendre de Chantilly au XVIIIe siècle: Héritages des manufactures de Rouen, Saint-Cloud et Paris et influences sur les autres manufactures du XVIIIe siècle* (Paris: Hazan, 1996).

11. Vincennes came under royal patronage outright in 1751, following the death of Orry de Fulvy; it was then relocated to Sèvres in 1756. On the critical fortunes of the manufactory, see Tamara Préaud and Antoine d'Albis, *La Porcelaine des Vincennes* (Paris: Adam Biro, 1991).

12. Hellman, "The Nature of Artifice," 43.

13. Ibid.

14. Ibid., 54–55. See also Katie Scott, "Framing Ambition: The Interior Politics of Madame de Pompadour," *Art History* 28 (2) (May 2005): 266–75.

especially when we consider the identity of the sitter.[15] One needs only to think of the story of how Pompadour filled the hothouse at Bellevue with bouquets from Vincennes to realize that porcelain was an integral part of her self-fashioning as well as her reputation for profuse consumption.[16] Indeed, the longer one looks, the clearer it becomes that the rose in Boucher's portrait must go by another name.

The Challenge of Color

To better understand the role of color in this discussion, let us step back to consider the state of French porcelain in the early 1750s. While the secret to hard-paste porcelain had been cracked by a group of individuals associated with the Dresden court of Augustus the Strong in 1708–9, French artisans remained largely unaware of the fact that "true" porcelain consists of a mixture of kaolin, quartz, and feldspar.[17] Following the longstanding (and false) idea that it is akin to glass, they instead continued to add ground glass or frit to their clay, thereby forming a composite known as soft-paste porcelain.[18] While soft-paste porcelain was generally considered inferior in quality to wares made in China or at Meissen, it did enjoy one distinct advantage: the lower firing temperatures (1100°C/2000°F versus 1400°C/2500°F) allowed for decoration with a much broader range of colors, as most known colorants would begin to vitrify (bleed out) at the high temperatures required for making hard-paste porcelain.[19]

In 1745, Louis XV demonstrated a nascent understanding of the inherent potential of soft-paste porcelain by

15. Charlotte Paludan, "A Beguiling Similarity: A Contribution to the History of Artificial Flowers," in *Flowers into Art: Floral Motifs in European Painting and Decorative Arts*, ed. Vibeke Woldbye (The Hague: SDU Publishers, 1991), 116–26.

16. The story of Pompadour's hothouse is repeated in many sources without any citation of a primary source. To date, the earliest reference I have found is William M. Chaffers, *Marks and Monograms on Pottery and Porcelain of the Renaissance and Modern Periods*, 4th ed. (London: Bickers & Son, 1874), 581. See Ewa Lajer-Burcharth, *The Painter's Touch: Boucher, Chardin, Fragonard* (Princeton, N.J.: Princeton University Press, 2018), 80–83.

17. The individuals in question were Ehrenfried Walther von Tschirnhaus, Johann Friedrich Böttger, and Gottfried Pabst von Ohain. For more on the role of each in the invention of hard-paste porcelain in Europe, see Schönfeld, "Was There a Western Inventor of Porcelain?"

18. Antoine d'Albis, "The Vincennes-Sèvres Factory and the Quest for Hard-Paste Porcelain 1747–1768," *The French Porcelain Society* 8 (1998): 1–29. Hard-paste porcelain was produced for the first time in France at the Sèvres manufactory in the 1770s.

19. The best introduction to the chemistry of porcelain production remains W. David Kingery and Pamela B. Vandiver, *Ceramic Masterpieces: Art, Structure and Technology* (New York: Free Press, 1986). For the advantages of lower firing temperatures, see pp. 269–72.

granting Vincennes the exclusive right to produce French porcelain for twenty-five years. Designed to stave off competition from other local manufactories, the royal order simultaneously called upon artisans at Vincennes to produce porcelain "in the manner of Saxony, painted and gilded with figures"—that is, to create porcelain as vibrant as the wares from Meissen.[20] During the thirty-five years that it had been in operation, Meissen had gained a European-wide reputation for producing the whitest paste and the most brilliant colors. While the first attribute is readily traced to the kaolin deposits that had been found in nearby Colditz in 1708, achieving the latter was a much more protracted affair.[21] The first colored enamel that the manufactory put into production took nearly a decade to develop, and it was an additional twenty years before it could be employed with any degree of certainty.[22] The key ingredient, cobalt, resulted in a brilliant, royal blue, imitating the blue and white ware from China that was so popular among European collectors (Fig. 3).[23]

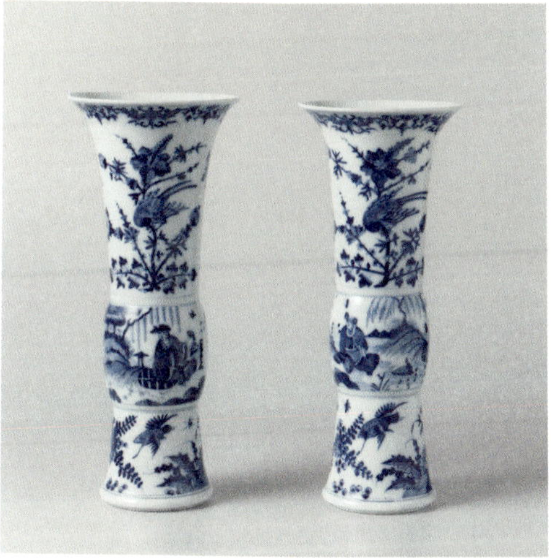

Fig. 3
Manufactured by Meissen Porcelain Manufactory, *Two Vases*, c. 1725. Hard-paste porcelain, height: 30.8 cm; diameter: 13.7 cm. Rijksmuseum, Amsterdam, BK-17334-A/B.

Painted under a translucent glaze that was added after the initial firing of an object, this blue was not only the first color employed at Meissen, but also its first underglaze enamel.[24] Due to the high firing temperature of the glaze, most colors developed at the manufactory were

20. Préaud and d'Albis, *La Porcelaine des Vincennes*, 37–51.

21. Schönfeld, "Was There a Western Inventor of Porcelain?" 725.

22. Martin Mields, "Die Entwicklung der Aufglassurpalette des europäischen Hartporzellans bis 1731 mit besonderen Berücksichtigung der Arbeiten von Johann Gregorius Höroldt," *Kermaische Zeitschrift* 8 (1963): 453–59.

23. On the early modern mining and preparation of cobalt, see Barbara H. Berrie, "Mining for Color: New Blues, Yellows, and Translucent Paint," in *Early Modern Color Worlds*, ed. Tawrin Baker, Sven Dupré, Sachiko Kusukawa, and Karin Leonhard (Leiden, Netherlands: Brill, 2016), 20–46. For blue and white ware, see Anne Gerritsen, *The City of Blue and White: Chinese Porcelain and the Early Modern World* (Cambridge: Cambridge University Press, 2020)

24. Known as biscuit firing, the purpose of this initial firing is to sinter the components of porcelain together. The second, or glost firing, locks the glaze in place.

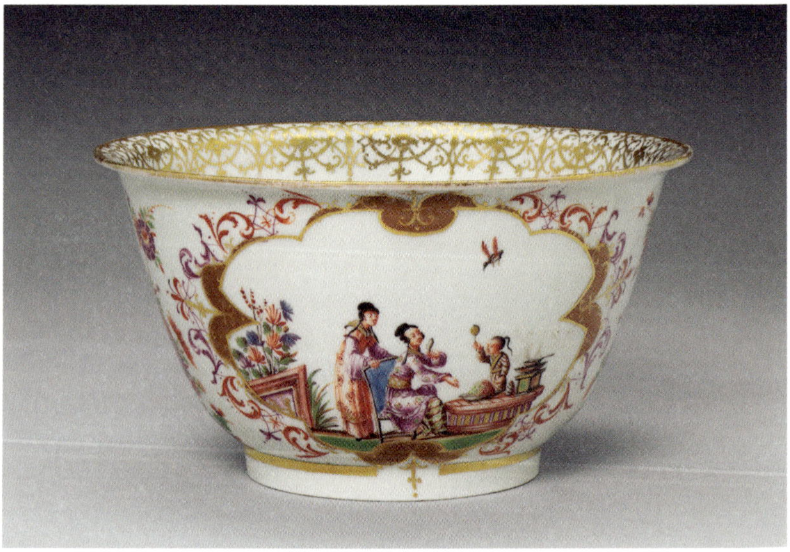

Fig. 4
Manufactured by Meissen Porcelain Manufactory, painted in the style of Johann Gregorius Höroldt, *Waste Bowl*, c. 1735. Hard-paste porcelain with polychrome enamel and gold, height: 8.3 cm; diameter: 17.1 cm. Harvard Art Museums/Busch-Reisinger Museum, Gift of Ilse Bischoff, BR58.29.

overglaze enamels. Like the example cited above, these enamels were comprised of colorants made with metal oxides and were adapted from recipes used in the decoration of other high-firing materials, such as metal and glass.[25] Among the many individuals who attempted to make these recipes suitable for porcelain, Johann Gregorius Höroldt deserves special mention. A wallpaper painter who had previously worked for the rival Du Paquier porcelain manufactory in Vienna, Höroldt succeeded in adding fifteen overglaze enamels to the manufactory's repertoire during his first ten years at Meissen.[26] Some of these enamels—namely, red (iron oxide), green (copper oxide), and black (manganese oxide)—can be seen on a waste bowl that dates to around 1735 and is now in the Harvard Art Museums (Fig. 4). Decorated

25. Mields, "Die Entwicklung der Aufglassurpalette des europäischen Hartporzellans bis 1731 mit besonderen Berücksichtigung der Arbeiten von Johann Gregorius Höroldt," 453.

26. Richard Seyffarth, "Johann Gregor Höroldt als Chemiker und Techniker," *Mitteilungsblatt Keramik-Freunde der Schweiz* 39 (1957): 22–25. Höroldt arrived at Meissen in the spring of 1720.

in a style that would become synonymous with Höroldt's name, the bowl presents the European fantasy of domestic life in China that remained a favorite theme among court circles for much of the eighteenth century.[27]

Transmuting Gold

Among the many colors on the Harvard waste bowl, the one most pertinent to this discussion is purple. Used both to represent the figures (particularly their garments) and in accompanying decorative elements, the purple seen on the bowl is not identical to the one that defines the rose in Boucher's portrait of Pompadour. Yet the same general recipe would have been used for both, if the rose is also made of porcelain. Commonly known as Purple of Cassius after the Leiden physician Andreas Cassius, who described it at length in his treatise *De Auro* (1685), the recipe had been known for about a generation to glassmakers, who used it to produce ruby red glass.[28] First, gold and tin are separately dissolved in aqua regia, a solution of nitric and hydrochloric acid. The two solutions are then mixed together and allowed to precipitate until a red substance forms, which is filtered out and used as a colorant.[29] Because of its ability to remain relatively stable under extreme heat, Purple of Cassius quickly became a color of choice for artisans working with high-firing materials.

The term "relatively" is used here with purpose: even the slightest change in how Purple of Cassius is prepared can drastically alter the outcome, as evidenced by the recipe for *aurum fulminans*. When gold is dissolved in aqua regia without the addition of tin, it results in a yellow precipitate that can become volatile and

27. For more on this phenomenon, commonly referred to as chinoiserie, see Madeleine Jarry, *Chinoiserie: Chinese Influence on European Decorative Art, 17th and 18th Centuries* (New York: Vendome Press, 1981).

28. Leslie B. Hunt, "The True Story of Purple of Cassius. The Birth of Gold-Based Glass and Enamel Colors," *Gold Bulletin* 9 (4) (December 1976): 134–39.

29. The synopsis of the recipe offered here is based on Sarah Lowengard, *The Creation of Color in Eighteenth-Century Europe* (New York: Columbia University Press, 2007). On the recipes for Purple of Cassius used at Meissen, see Nicholas Zumbulyadis, "'...with a dreadful bang!' A Chemical History of Böttger Lustre," *Keramos* 222 (2013): 3–16. On the recipes used at Vincennes and Sèvres, see Antoine d'Albis, "Les débuts de pourpres en France, de Chantilly à Vincennes: Salomon Taunay et son fils Pierre Henri Antoine," *Sèvres* 3 (1994): 34–37.

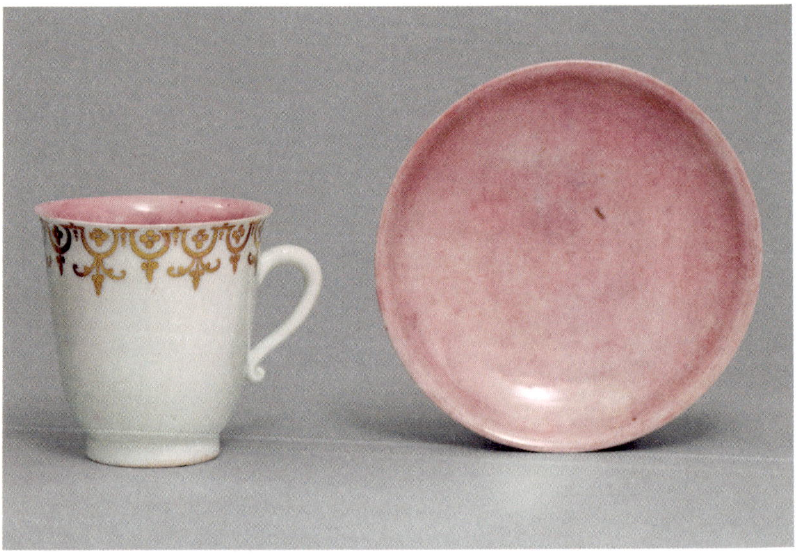

Fig. 5
Attributed to Johann Friedrich Böttger, manufactured by Meissen Porcelain Manufactory, *Cup and Saucer*, c. 1717–20. Hard-paste porcelain with gold, height (cup): 7 cm; diameter (saucer): 11.4 cm. Metropolitan Museum of Art, New York, Gift of R. Thornton Wilson, in memory of Florence Ellsworth Wilson, 1954, 54.147.83, .84.

explode if exposed to heat.[30] A coffee cup and saucer now in the Metropolitan Museum of Art in New York (Fig. 5) show that *aurum fulminans* was nevertheless used in the decoration of porcelain.[31] Attributed to Johann Friedrich Böttger, one of the "inventors" of European porcelain, the cup and saucer were made at Meissen during the first decade of the manufactory's operation and represent an early attempt at a luster, a form of overglaze decoration composed of noble metals.[32] Böttger's success in tempering the explosive qualities of *aurum fulminans* is likely thanks to his training as an alchemist, a kind of early modern expert with a special interest in the properties of gold.[33] While his results may be disappointing aesthetically (the luster is concentrated unevenly in areas on both

30. Nicholas Zumbulyadis, "Decorating with Explosives: The Use of *Aurum Fulminans* as a Purple Pigment," *Bulletin for the History of Chemistry* 39 (1) (2014): 7 17.

31. This was made possible by adding sulfur to the resultant precipitate, lessening its susceptibility to heat.

32. Kingery and Vandiver, *Ceramic Masterpieces*, 261–77.

33. The secret of transmutation, or the ability to turn base metals into gold, was sought after by alchemists, who believed the procedure hinged on a material called the philosopher's stone. Glenn Adamson, "Rethinking the Arcanum: Porcelain, Secrecy, and the Eighteenth-Century Culture of Invention," in Cavanaugh and Yonan, *The Cultural Aesthetics of Eighteenth-Century Porcelain*, 19–38.

cup and saucer), they are significant for what they reveal about the making of pink: an optical illusion, pink is conjured here by the refraction of light off nanoparticles of gold, which is registered by the human eye in the red region of the visible spectrum.[34]

Whether the artisans who worked in Europe's earliest porcelain manufactories were aware of the optics of color is unclear. Regardless, they knew that by altering the quantity and/or quality of certain colorants they could radically change the appearance of an object. It was common knowledge, for example, that gold could result in pink, purple, red, or royal blue, and that a higher concentration of the metal would generally yield a darker color. But this was not easy to control: the concentration of gold depended on how many layers of the corresponding enamel or luster were present, the amount of gold that had been precipitated, and the purity of the gold itself.[35] Similarly, while certain colorants react in one way upon one kind of substrate, the same colorants might react in a completely different manner upon another. Soft-paste porcelain, for example, tends to absorb gold-based colorants into its body, which makes it impossible to achieve the same effect as seen on hard-paste porcelain.[36] This might explain the unusual, purple color of the rose in Boucher's portrait of Pompadour, or why the manufactory at Vincennes tested dozens of recipes for gold-based colorants before arriving at a satisfactory solution.[37]

34. Lowengard, *The Creation of Color in Eighteenth-Century Europe*.

35. Marino Magetti and Antoine d'Albis, "Phase and Compositional Analysis of a Sèvres Soft-Paste Porcelain Plate from 1781, with a Review of Early Porcelain Techniques," *European Journal of Mineralogy* 29 (3) (June 2017): 2.

36. Ibid.

37. For a good overview of the struggle to find a viable gold-based colorant at Vincennes, see Susan M. Wager, "Almost an Original: Eighteenth-Century French Porcelain and the Materiality of Production," in *Colour Histories: Science, Art, and Technology in the 17th and 18th Centuries*, ed. Magdalena Bushart and Friedrich Steinle (Berlin: De Gruyter, 2015), 115–28. I am grateful to Sarah Lowengard for generously sharing with me her transcription of the contents of Carton Y.51 at the Archives de la manufacture nationale de Sèvres (AMNS).

"Painting" Porcelain

The tactic adopted at Vincennes was to leave certain colorants in a powdered state and to dust them onto the surface of the object with a sieve, as opposed to the typical method of mixing them with an oily substance and applying them with a brush.[38] Dusting allowed the colorant to melt both into and onto the substrate on which it was applied, creating a wonderfully saturated effect that can be seen on a tray in the Wadsworth Atheneum in Hartford, Connecticut (Fig. 6).[39] Dated around 1757–58, the tray marks a new era in the production of French porcelain, both because it was the product of the recently opened Royal Porcelain Manufactory at Sèvres and because it featured one of the many ground colors—*fond rose*—that would become a hallmark of the

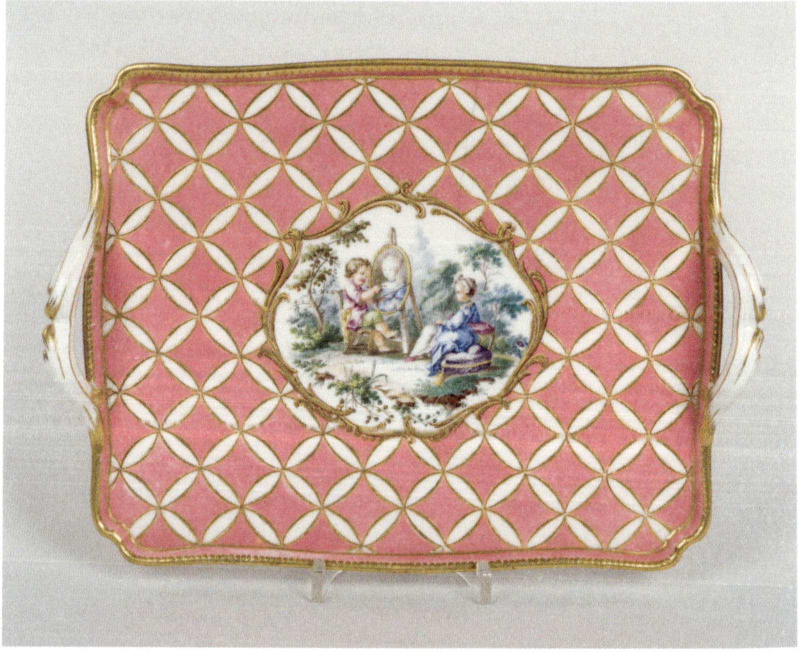

Fig.6
Painted by Andre-Vincent Vieillard, manufactured by Sèvres Manufactory, *Tray*, 1757–58. Soft-paste porcelain with polychrome enamel and gold, 33.1 × 23.2 cm. Wadsworth Atheneum Museum of Art, Hartford, Conn., Gift of J. Pierpont Morgan, 1917.1006.

38. This decision was reached in 1752, one year after the appointment of chemist Jean Hellot as the manufactory's chief technical advisor. For more on Hellot, see Raffaele Pisano, "Jean Hellot and Eighteenth-Century Chemistry at the Service of the State," in *A Bridge Between Conceptual Frameworks: Sciences, Society and Technology Studies*, ed. Raffaele Pisano (Dodrecht, Netherlands: Springer, 2015), 179–93.

39. Linda H. Roth and Clare Le Corbeiller, *French Eighteenth-Century Porcelain at the Wadsworth Atheneum: The J. Pierpont Morgan Collection* (Hartford, Conn.: Wadsworth Atheneum, 2000), 176.

site.[40] While Pompadour's part in the foundation of Sèvres has been widely debated by scholars, her role in elevating its wares to the height of fashion and good taste is without question.[41] Some authors have gone so far as to dub the ground color seen on this tray *rose Pompadour* based on the erroneous assumption that the color was Pompadour's favorite. Scholars have also tried to make a case for its presence in Harvard's Boucher portrait—in the background of the cameo of Louis XV or as subtle references in her pink ribbons and blush.[42]

The rose in Boucher's painting, however, resists such interpretation. Considering Pompadour's well-known passion for porcelain and her interest in supporting local manufactories, it is productive to read its unusual hue as a reflection of the ongoing efforts of French porcelain makers to improve their wares and thereby surpass their foreign rivals. Neither a traditional allegory of beauty nor a simple hair dressing, the rose in Boucher's portrait of Madame de Pompadour is a singular statement about the past and future of French porcelain.

Gabriella Szalay is a Ph.D. candidate at the Georg-August-Universität Göttingen; she served as the 2018–20 Renke B. and Pamela M. Thye Curatorial Fellow in the Busch-Reisinger Museum.

40. The complicated history of the relocation of the Vincennes manufactory to Sèvres is beyond the scope of this essay. For more on this topic and a good primer on the various ground colors introduced at Sèvres, see Svend Eriksen and Geoffrey de Bellaigue, *Sèvres Porcelain: Vincennes and Sèvres 1740–1800*, trans. R. J. Charleston (London: Faber & Faber, 1987).

41. Even Donald Posner, who famously challenged Pompadour's role as a patron of the arts, did not deny her importance in making the wares of Vincennes and later Sèvres must-have items. Donald Posner, "Mme. de Pompadour as a Patron of the Visual Arts," *The Art Bulletin* 72 (1) (March 1990): 74–105.

42. It seems that Pompadour's favorite color for porcelain was blue. See Marie-Laure de Rochebrune, "La passion de madame de Pompadour pour la porcelaine," in *Madame de Pompadour et les Arts*, ed. Xavier Salmon (Paris: Réunion des musées nationaux, 2002), 411. For the complex historiography of *rose Pompadour*, see Christine A. Jones, *Shapely Bodies: The Image of Porcelain in Eighteenth-Century France* (Newark: University of Delaware Press, 2013), 231, no. 72. Another recent publication that identifies *rose Pompadour* in Boucher's portrait of Pompadour is Ewa Lajer-Burcharth, "Pompadour's Touch: Difference in Representation," *Representations* 73 (1) (Winter 2001): 74–77.

Making Up Race

Whiteness, Pinkness, and Pompadour

Oliver Wunsch

BOUCHER'S PORTRAIT OF MADAME de Pompadour revolves around the subject of skin color. Originally conceived as a small portrait closely framed around the face of the royal mistress, it was enlarged a short time later into a more complex composition depicting Pompadour as she applies her rouge. These additions, likely carried out by Boucher himself, were ostensibly meant to cover up damage that the painting had sustained in transit.[1] More than a practical repair, however, the changes raise larger questions about the presentation of skin in the middle of the eighteenth century—and about the significance of pink skin in particular.

The role of cosmetics in Boucher's painting has long interested art historians, who have pointed out the connection that the portrait implies between makeup and paint. For Melissa Hyde, the portrait is a response to period critics who regarded both paint and makeup as tools of social duplicity; Boucher and Pompadour, Hyde argues, proudly declare themselves tricksters, embracing artifice as an essential component of creative expression.[2] Ewa Lajer-Burcharth has further emphasized how Pompadour's use of makeup registers her material role in fabricating her own image, with artist and subject acting as co-creators.[3]

But for all the attention that scholars have devoted to the painting's treatment of makeup, surprisingly little has been said

1. Alden R. Gordon and Teri Hensick, "The Picture within the Picture: Boucher's 1750 Portrait of Madame de Pompadour Identified," *Apollo* 155 (480) (February 2002): 21–30.

2. Melissa Hyde, "The 'Makeup' of the Marquise: Boucher's Portrait of Pompadour at Her Toilette," *The Art Bulletin* 82 (3) (September 2000): 453–75.

3. Ewa Lajer-Burcharth, "Pompadour's Touch: Difference in Representation," *Representations* 73 (1) (Winter 2001): 54–88.

about questions of skin color. What was the significance of pink skin in the mid-eighteenth century? And what might it mean to display oneself in the act of *constructing* that pinkness?

These questions gain urgency when we consider the historical setting. The eighteenth century marked a moment of profound transformation in the way Europeans understood the meaning of skin color. Complexion, which had historically been regarded as a marker of gender and class, was now seen in a broader geographic context. At a time when Europeans were enslaving millions of African people to support their overseas colonies, they began to incorporate skin color into new theories of physiological difference—ones that they could invoke as justification for their actions.[4]

These ideas did not emerge overnight, nor did they displace the old values and associations that Europeans had attached to complexion. On the contrary, as recent scholarship on the history of race has shown, eighteenth-century conceptions of skin color were defined by their instability and heterogeneity.[5] It was, in fact, the confusion and incipient status of this racial consciousness that allowed artists to play a role in shaping it.[6]

This essay situates Boucher's portrait of Pompadour within the eighteenth century's evolving conception of skin color. After placing the portrait in the context of period commentary on pink skin, I examine how Pompadour's distinctive identity—as a bourgeoise with intimate knowledge of the French slave trade—suggests what skin color might have meant to her in particular. Finally, I compare Boucher's portrait with another painting that Pompadour commissioned of herself at the same moment, one that shows how she repeatedly used art to play with the status and privilege afforded by her complexion.

4. For the French racialization of skin color as a justification for slavery, see especially Pierre H. Boulle, *Race et esclavage dans la France de l'Ancien Régime* (Paris: Perrin, 2007); and Andrew S. Curran, *The Anatomy of Blackness: Science and Slavery in an Age of Enlightenment* (Baltimore: Johns Hopkins University Press, 2011).

5. Roxann Wheeler, in particular, has emphasized this point; see Roxann Wheeler, *The Complexion of Race: Categories of Difference in Eighteenth-Century British Culture* (Philadelphia: University of Pennsylvania Press, 2000). In a French context, Andrew Curran has similarly drawn attention to the instability of eighteenth-century conceptions of race; see Curran, *The Anatomy of Blackness*.

6. For two recent studies that begin to address the role that artists played in constructing period ideas about skin color, see Anne Lafont, *L'art et la race: L'Africain (tout) contre l'œil des Lumières* (Dijon: Les presses du réel, 2019); and Mechthild Fend, *Fleshing out Surfaces: Skin in French Art and Medicine, 1650–1850* (Manchester: Manchester University Press, 2017).

Makeup and skin, of course, are not the same thing. Makeup is a medium of perfection that serves, in the words of the *Encyclopédie*, "to embellish ... to repair by artifice."[7] But this aspirational quality of makeup is precisely what makes it a revealing indication of the values that a society attaches to skin itself. To understand what it meant for Pompadour to paint herself pink, we therefore need to begin by examining how her makeup relates to the deeper dermal fantasies of her time.

White and pink cosmetics were, in and of themselves, nothing new. The practice of using white and red substances to color the face dates at least to Greek and Roman antiquity.[8] In the Classical world, white complexion was correlated with social status, an indication that one did not need to work in the sun for a living.[9] Pink, in this context, served to highlight the whiteness of the surrounding skin by way of contrast and to prevent the face from acquiring a lifeless pallor.[10] These associations persisted into the early modern period, when white and pink cosmetics were essential accessories for anyone wishing to appear in European court society.[11]

While the basic palette of the face remained relatively consistent among the European elite, the ideas associated with these colors evolved. One significant factor was social mobility. The spread of luxury markets and the rise of bourgeois consumption meant that cosmetics once associated with noble status became a less reliable indicator of social rank.[12] Makeup had always been subject to ridicule as a medium of deceit, especially as a tool of feminine duplicity, but by the end of the seventeenth century it was increasingly regarded as a means of class dissimulation.[13] By the mid-eighteenth century, artist Charles-Nicolas Cochin wondered why rouge carried any social value at all when it was affordable across classes: "It is astonishing that we

7. "Embellir...réparer par artifice." Louis de Jaucourt, "Fard," in *Encyclopédie, ou dictionnaire raisonné des sciences, des arts et des métiers*, vol. 6 (Paris: Briasson, 1756), 408; translation mine.

8. Mireille M. Lee, *Body, Dress, and Identity in Ancient Greece* (New York: Cambridge University Press, 2015), 66–69; and Kelly Olson, "Cosmetics in Roman Antiquity: Substance, Remedy, Poison," *The Classical World* 102 (3) (2009): 291–310.

9. Lee, *Body, Dress, and Identity in Ancient Greece*, 67; and Olson, "Cosmetics in Roman Antiquity," 294–95.

10. In addition to the sources cited above, see Michael Hendry, "Rouge and Crocodile Dung: Notes on Ovid, Ars 3.199–200 and 269–70," *The Classical Quarterly* 45 (2) (1995): 583–88.

11. Catherine Lanoë, *La poudre et le fard: Une histoire des cosmétiques de la Renaissance aux Lumières* (Paris: Champ Vallon, 2008), 27–77.

12. Ibid., 278–79; and Lynn Festa, "Cosmetic Differences: The Changing Faces of England and France," *Studies in Eighteenth-Century Culture* 34 (1) (2005): 38.

13. On the long history of gender in anti-cosmetic discourse, see Jacqueline Lichtenstein, "Making Up Representation: The Risks of Femininity," *Representations*

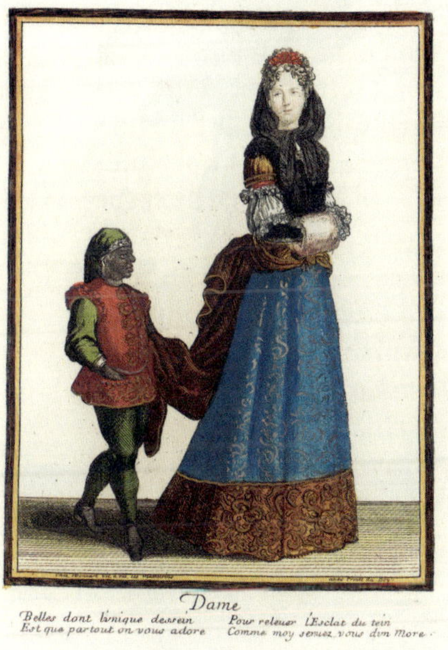

Fig. 1
Henri Bonnart, *Dame*, 1677, from *Recueil des modes de la cour de France* (Collection of Fashion from the Court of France), album compiled by an unidentified collector, c. 1702–4. Hand-colored engraving on paper, 36.51 × 23.81 cm. Los Angeles County Museum of Art, Purchased with funds provided by The Eli and Edythe L. Broad Foundation, Mr. and Mrs. H. Tony Oppenheimer, Mr. and Mrs. Reed Oppenheimer, Hal Oppenheimer, Alice and Nahum Lainer, Mr. and Mrs. Gerald Oppenheimer, Ricki and Marvin Ring, Mr. and Mrs. David Sydorick, the Costume Council Fund, and member of the Costume Council, M.2002.57.20.

have attached this distinction to a color that is so common and so cheap that the smallest *grisettes* can make this expenditure as copiously as a person of the highest birth."[14] He went on to joke that the truly wealthy might consider painting their cheeks with a more expensive color, such as ultramarine blue, to distinguish themselves.[15]

As the class connotations of makeup became more muddled, pink skin acquired another source of prestige. With Europeans expanding their geographic horizons and imperial ambitions, they began to judge their complexion in relation to people on distant continents. French women, for example, started to highlight the whiteness of their complexion by contrasting it with the skin of African people they enslaved.[16] The inscription on a fashion plate from the late seventeenth century (Fig. 1) makes the strategy explicit:

> Beauties whose unique aspiration
> Is for you to be everywhere adored
> To raise the brilliance of your complexion
> Make use, like I do, of a blackmoor.[17]

Much like using rouge to showcase the whiteness of the surrounding face, the enslaved boy here acts as a foil to a white ideal. The device became a familiar trope in French and British portraiture, deployed by artists from Pierre Mignard (Fig. 2) to Joshua Reynolds (Fig. 3).

20 (Fall 1987): 77–87.

14. "Il est étonnant qu'on ait attaché cette distinction à une couleur qui est si commune et à si bon marché, que les plus petites grisettes pourraient faire cette dépense aussi abondamment qu'une personne de la plus haute naissance." Charles-Nicolas Cochin, "Avis aux Dames," *Mercure de France*, May 1755, 130; translation mine.

15. Ibid.

16. For an overview of the topic, see David Bindman and Helen Weston, "Court and City: Fantasies of Domination," in *The Image of the Black in Western Art*, vol. 3, pt. 3, ed. David Bindman and Henry Louis Gates, Jr. (Cambridge, Mass.: Harvard University Press, 2011), 125–70.

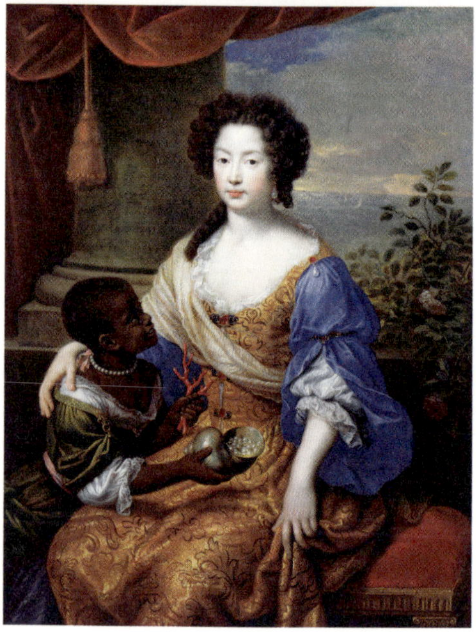

Fig. 2
Pierre Mignard, *Louise de Kéroualle, Duchess of Portsmouth with an unknown female attendant*, 1682. Oil on canvas, 120.7 × 95.3 cm. National Portrait Gallery, London, Purchased, 1878, NPG 497.

European men, too, commissioned portraits of themselves with enslaved people, but it was in depictions of women that the genre was most expressly linked to questions of beauty and complexion. The format was sometimes incorporated into a toilette scene, in which the white woman attempts to lighten the skin of her enslaved attendant by washing him (Fig. 4). Such portraits referenced the French proverbial saying "to whiten a Moor," which meant "to attempt the impossible."[18] Cosmetics might be capable of masking class distinctions, but the futile effort to whiten dark skin was meant to demonstrate the limits of what could be accomplished through rituals of the toilette. Some bodily distinctions, according to the racist logic of such images, are too great to overcome.

Boucher's painting of Pompadour does not belong to this overtly racist genre. One might even ask whether it has any connection to race at all. Historians of eighteenth-century art have tended to interpret portraits through a racial lens only when these works depict people of color. Portrayals of white people are implicitly seen as race neutral.[19] And yet, just as a portrait of a solitary man can say something about masculinity, a portrait of a white person alone can deliver a message about race. Unsealing that message requires us to look more closely at both the painting itself and the background of the person at its center.

First, what Boucher's painting shows us: Pompadour sits at a mirror, in the midst of applying her

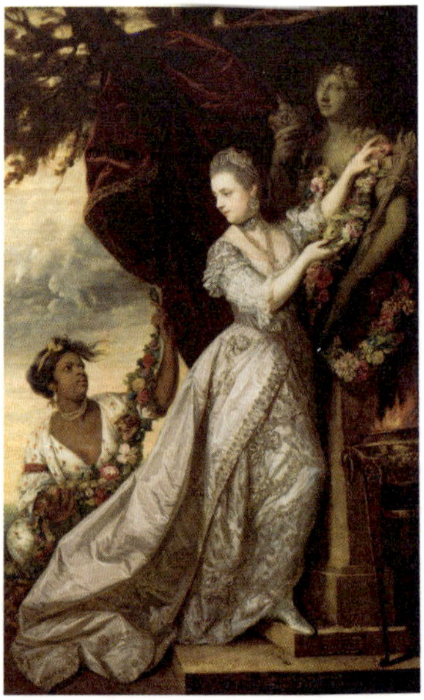

Fig. 3
Joshua Reynolds, *Portrait of Lady Elizabeth Keppel*, 1761. Oil on canvas, 236 × 146 cm. Woburn Abbey, Collection of the Duke of Bedford.

17. With modern French orthography: "Belles dont l'unique dessein / Est que partout on vous adore / Pour relever l'éclat du teint / Comme moi servez-vous d'un More." Translation mine.

18. Jean Michel Massing, "From Greek Proverb to Soap Advert: Washing the Ethiopian," *Journal of the Warburg and Courtauld Institutes* 58 (1995): 180–201.

19. For a notable exception, see Angela Rosenthal, "Visceral Culture: Blushing and the Legibility of Whiteness in Eighteenth-Century British Portraiture," *Art History* 24 (4) (2004): 563–92.

makeup. In one hand, she holds her *boîte à rouge*, a small container for storing the reddish-pink makeup that gives her cheeks their rosy hue (see p. 14). In the other, she gently clasps a *brosse à rouge*, a newly fashionable accessory that allowed for the precise application of makeup (p. 3).[20] On the table, we find her *boîte à poudre*, its top ajar (p. 13). Pompadour, it seems, has already used the feather brush on top—made from the finest down—to powder her face a brilliant white.[21] These accoutrements, which represent the latest trends in the cosmetics market, signal Pompadour's embrace of France's expanding consumer economy.

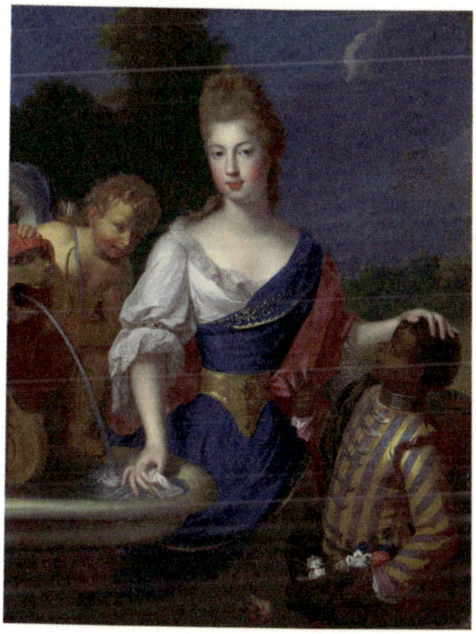

Fig. 4
Pierre Gobert, *Portrait of a lady, three-quarter-length, traditionally identified as Louise Bernardine de Durfort, Duchess of Duras (1678–1747), with Cupid and a page, by a fountain*, c. 1695–1700. Oil on canvas, 127.7 × 100 cm. Private collection.

Biographies of Pompadour frequently emphasize how she brought the sensibility of a bourgeoise to Versailles, solidifying bonds between the monarchy and France's ascendant financial elite.[22] The array of luxury goods in the toilette scene no doubt speaks to this class identity. They signal, as Melissa Hyde has observed, how Pompadour shrewdly performed her role as an arriviste at court, deploying fine cosmetics in a carefully calibrated social act.[23] But the significance of these commodities is not simply a matter of class status. They also point to France's increasingly global cosmetics industry, hinting at worlds far beyond the confines of Versailles.

Rouge in particular was a product of international commerce. Europeans had created versions of the cosmetic from locally available materials such as alkanet dye and iron oxide since antiquity, but by the sixteenth century, these materials began to compete with more exotic ingredients. Pernambuco wood from Brazil,

20. Lanoë, *La poudre et le fard*, 61.

21. Powder puffs—or *houppes*, as they were known—were typically made of either eiderdown or another light bird feather. Denis Diderot, "Houppe," in *Encyclopédie, ou dictionnaire raisonné des sciences, des arts et des métiers*, vol. 8 (Paris: Briasson, 1765), 326.

22. See, for example, Danielle Gallet-Guerne, *Madame de Pompadour, ou, Le pouvoir féminin* (Paris: Fayard, 1985).

23. Hyde, "The 'Makeup' of the Marquise."

sandalwood from Southeast Asia, and cochineal from Mexico and Central America all found their way onto the cheeks of European women.[24] These materials ranged in both color and price. Pernambuco wood was among the cheaper options but tended to yield a less saturated rouge than other sources. Cochineal, the insect from which carmine is derived, produced a much more vibrant hue but was exceptionally expensive.[25] The materials traveled thousands of miles to reach European shores, becoming an integral part of the triangle trade that linked Europe, Africa, and the Americas.[26]

More than most people at the time, Pompadour was well situated to understand the workings of this economy. Her upbringing and personal fortunes were intimately tied to French colonialism, particularly the institution of slavery that undergirded it. Her legal guardian and surrogate father, Charles-François Lenormant de Tournehem, was a director of the Compagnie des Indes, which oversaw the French slave trade throughout much of the eighteenth century.[27] Her godfather, financier Jean Pâris de Monmartel, was one of the principal sponsors of the slave trading company known as the Société d'Angole, providing nearly 20 percent of the capital for the group's formation in 1748.[28] These actions were part of a broader expansion of French investment in slavery during the first half of the eighteenth century. French traders abducted approximately five thousand people from Africa each year in the 1710s; by the late 1730s, the number of people forced onto French ships had soared above eighteen thousand.[29] At mid century, France sent an average of fifty-five ships on slaving missions every year, each ship commonly transporting more than two hundred fifty enslaved people.[30] On average, one in seven people died during the course of the voyage.[31]

24. Lanoë, *La poudre et le fard*, 53–57.

25. Ibid., 56.

26. Emily Lynn Osborn, "Red Echoes of Enslavement: Cochineal Red, West Africa, and the Slave Trade," in *A Red Like No Other: How Cochineal Colored the World: An Epic Story of Art, Culture, Science, and Trade*, ed. Carmella Padilla and Barbara Anderson (New York: Skira/Rizzoli, 2015), 82–87; and James E. McClellan III, *Colonialism and Science: Saint Domingue in the Old Regime* (Baltimore: Johns Hopkins University Press, 1992), 152–55.

27. Philippe Haudrère, "L'origine du personnel de direction générale de la Compagnie française des Indes, 1719–1794," *Revue française d'histoire d'outre-mer* 67 (248) (1980): 354. The Compagnie des Indes held a monopoly on French commerce on the African coast from 1720 to 1767. During this period, it outfitted its own slave ships while also selling slaving licenses to other companies. Pierre Dardel, *Navires et marchandises dans les ports de Rouen et du Havre au XVIIIe siècle* (Paris: SEVPEN, 1963), 137.

28. André Delcourt, *La France et les établissements français au Sénégal entre 1713 et 1763* (Dakar: IFAN, 1952), 75. Monmartel invested 375,000 livres of the total two million livres invested in the company at its inception. Gaston Martin, *Nantes au XVIIIe siècle: L'ère des négriers* (Paris: F. Alcan, 1931), 250–51.

If Pompadour's upbringing did not alert her to this economy, then her ascent to the halls of royal power surely did. By 1748, a new slave ship had been christened in her honor, and another vessel would be named for her in the coming years.[32] In 1749, she and Louis XV visited the port city of Le Havre, where Pompadour placed a ceremonial peg in a newly commissioned 320-ton slave ship named *Le Gracieux*.[33] And in her personal retinue, Pompadour herself held "two negroes," as they were described in an account of her expenses.[34]

These injustices might seem far removed from the world of Pompadour's toilette. But in a colonial economy in which skin colorants traveled to Europe aboard the same ships that transported enslaved people across the Atlantic, the two domains were intimately intertwined. And in a society that sought to rationalize these injustices through the nascent pseudoscience of skin color, the brutality of slavery and the refinement of the toilette were more closely linked than we might think.

Pompadour did not, so far as we know, record any reflections on skin color in writing. Our main guide to her understanding of skin color comes from the works of art that she commissioned. In this respect, it is helpful, by way of conclusion, to compare Boucher's portrait with a different painting commissioned by

29. Robert Louis Stein, *The French Slave Trade in the Eighteenth Century: An Old Regime Business* (Madison: University of Wisconsin Press, 1979), 211.

30. Ibid., 27.

31. Olivier Pétré-Grenouilleau, *Les traites négrières: Essai d'histoire globale* (Paris: Gallimard, 2004), 140.

32. For the first ship, see Éric Saugera, *Bordeaux, port négrier: Chronologie, économie, idéologie, XVIIe–XIXe siècles* (Biarritz: J & D éditions, 1995), 303–4, 352. The 150-ton ship was in service by November 1748. Jean Mettas, *Répertoire des expéditions négrières françaises au XVIIIe siècle*, vol. 2 (Paris: Société française d'histoire d'outre-mer, 1984), 24. The second ship, listed at 260 tons, was registered at the port of Le Havre in 1753 under the ownership of Jean Féray, a well-known slave trader. Dardel, *Navires et marchandises dans les ports de Rouen et du Havre au XVIIIe siècle*, 527. It was seized by the British Navy in 1756 on its way back to Le Havre from Martinique during the blockade instituted in the course of the Seven Years' War. *The Gentleman's Magazine* 26 (1756): 452.

33. The ceremony was described at the time by the Marquis d'Argenson; see René-Louis de Voyer, Marquis d'Argenson, *Mémoires et journal inédit du marquis d'Argenson, ministre des affaires étrangères sous Louis XV*, vol. 3 (1857), 288. Edouard Delobette has identified the ship in the maritime records of the Archives départementales de Seine-Maritime, where it is listed under the ownership of Jean Féray; see Edouard Delobette, "Négociants et traite des Noirs au Havre au XVIIIe siècle," *Annales de Normandie* 48 (3) (1998): 294n107. Tonnage, in the context of eighteenth-century nautical records, does not measure a ship's weight but the volume of its cargo-carrying capacity. At the time, one ton translated to 1.44 cubic meters. Stein, *The French Slave Trade in the Eighteenth Century*, 70–71.

34. Pompadour did not specify their names, listing them simply as "deux nègres." "Relevé des dépenses de Madame de Pompadour," in *Mémoires de la Société des sciences morales, des lettres et des arts de Seine-et-Oise*, vol. 3 (1853), 144.

Fig. 5
Carle Vanloo, *Sultana Drinking Coffee*, 1755. Oil on canvas, 120 × 127 cm. State Hermitage Museum, Saint Petersburg, Entered the Hermitage in 1782, ГЭ-7489.

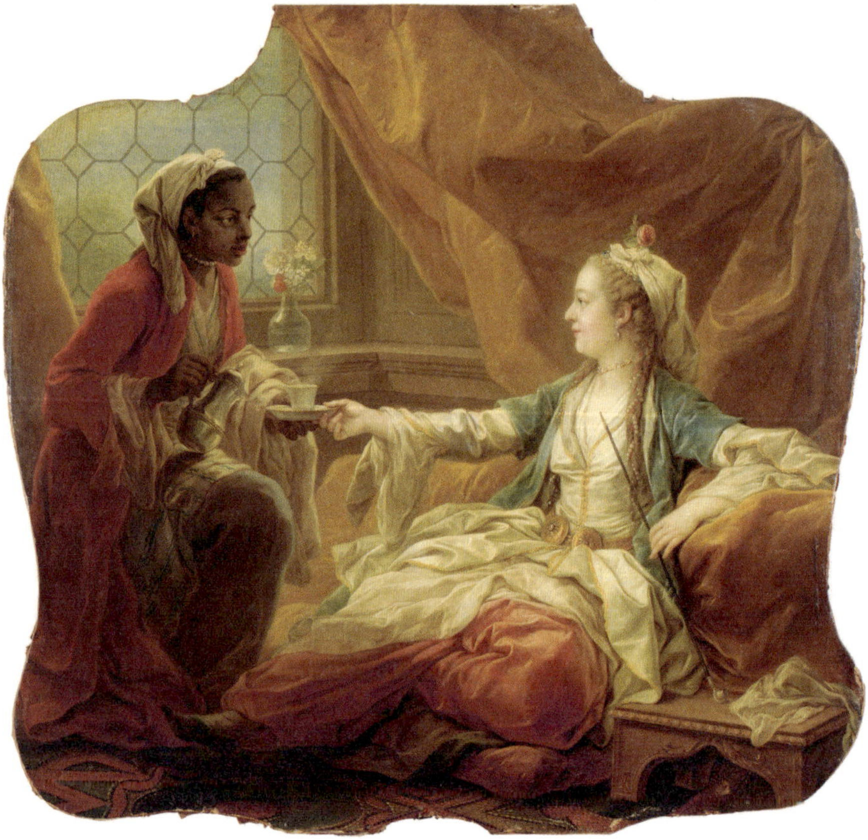

35. On the circumstances of the commission, see Perrin Stein, "Madame de Pompadour and the Harem Imagery at Bellevue," *Gazette des Beaux-Arts* 123 (January 1994): 29–44.

Pompadour, one that deals more explicitly with the place of skin color in global commerce (Fig. 5).

Painted in 1755 by Carle Vanloo, it depicts Pompadour in the guise of a sultana in a Middle Eastern harem, attended by a Black woman.[35] The painting was exhibited at the Salon the following year under the title *A Sultana Taking Coffee Presented to Her by a Negress*.[36] Viewers immediately recognized that the "sultana" was meant to represent Pompadour.[37]

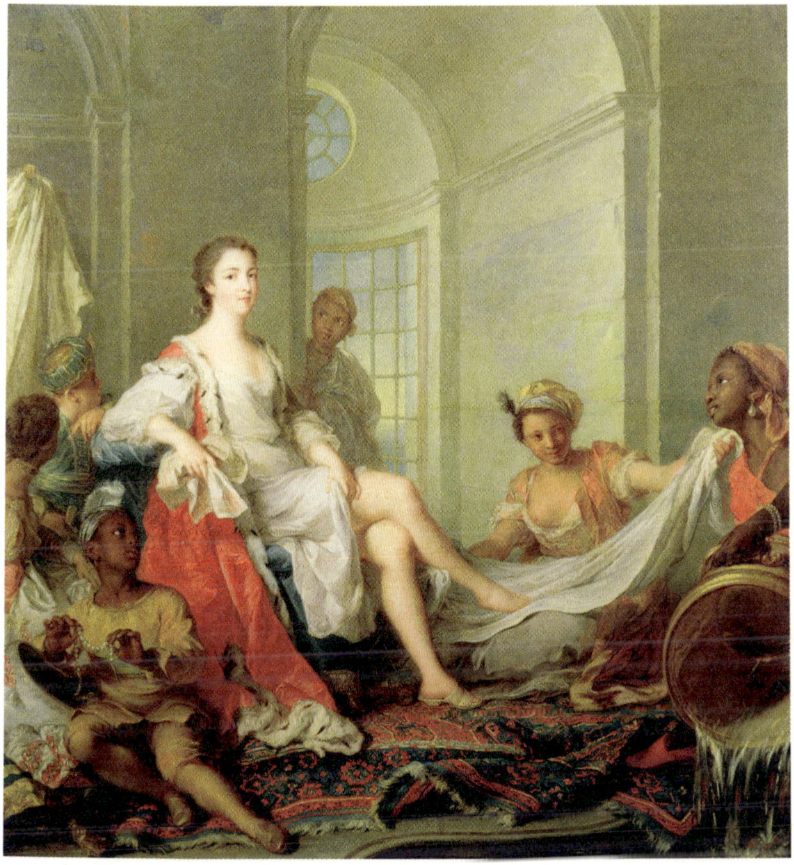

Fig. 6
Jean-Marc Nattier, *Mademoiselle de Clermont en Sultane* (Mademoiselle de Clermont as a Sultana), 1733. Oil on canvas, 109 × 104.5 cm. The Wallace Collection, London, P456.

The conceit was a familiar one. In the preceding decades, it had become fashionable for European women to commission portraits of themselves dressed *à la Turque*, often appearing alongside people of color who attend to their needs. The key elements of the genre were established by such well-known examples as Jean-Marc Nattier's *Mademoiselle de Clermont en Sultane* (Mademoiselle de Clermont as a Sultana; Fig. 6), in which dark-skinned figures dutifully serve their white mistress, gazing upon her with adoration.

36. *Explication des peintures, sculptures, et gravures de messieurs de l'Académie Royale* (1755), 9, no. 17.

37. Baillet de Saint-Julien, *Seconde lettre à un partisan du bon goût sur l'exposition des tableaux faite dans le grand Sallon du Louvre* (1755), 5; and Antoine-Nicolas Dezallier d'Argenville, *Voyage pittoresque des environs de Paris, ou Description des maisons royales, châteaux & autres lieux de plaisance, situés à quinze lieues aux environs de cette ville* (1755), 28.

Various commodities, from pearls to textiles, function as analogues to the white woman's skin, highlighting whiteness as a defining quality of beauty.

Vanloo's portrait of Pompadour compresses these metaphors into a single object: the coffee cup that passes between the women's hands. But here the metaphor carries a complex message. The painting invites us not only to connect the white ceramic cup with Pompadour's porcelain skin, but also to link the attendant's complexion with the black beverage that she serves. The analogy goes deeper than a simple visual comparison. Coffee, a newly fashionable luxury good harvested by enslaved people in European colonies, points both to the Black woman's skin color and to her transformation into a commodity traded across oceans.[38] White ceramic, too, carries a layered meaning in this context, Pompadour being an instrumental sponsor of French porcelain production.[39] Taken together, the analogies force us to consider both women—and skin colors—as products of commerce. There is no question, of course, that the painting positions the Black woman as subservient to Pompadour, doing little to challenge the hierarchies of skin color that Europeans were constructing at this time. But it also calls attention to the way these hierarchies were determined by commercial interests, how perceptions of bodily difference were conditioned by markets as much as they were determined by nature.

It is in this commercial understanding of skin that the harem scene sheds light on Boucher's portrait of Pompadour. Both paintings show an awareness of how complexion was being redefined through the logic of commerce—the way skin could be manufactured, packaged, and sold. During a period when Enlightenment naturalists and anatomists were searching for physiological explanations to bolster theories of racial difference, the paintings that Pompadour commissioned presented skin through an alternative lens.[40] The makeup that she applies to her face at her toilette, like the ceramic cup she holds in her hand in the harem, reminds

38. On the ties between coffee and slavery in the French Caribbean, see Michel-Rolph Trouillot, "Motion in the System: Coffee, Color, and Slavery in Eighteenth-Century Saint-Domingue," *Review* 5 (3) (Winter 1982): 331–88.

39. On this topic, see Gabriella Szalay's essay in this volume.

40. On the anatomical study of racial difference at this time, see especially Curran, *The Anatomy of Blackness*.

I would like to thank Cassandra Albinson, Soyoung Lee, Heather Linton, Sarah Kuschner, and Micah Buis for their suggestions and support in the development of this essay.

us that her whiteness is not a privilege accorded by nature, but a quality that is culturally produced, purchased, and staged.

Boucher's portrait has been celebrated as a canny performance of identity, a bold assertion of female autonomy and social mobility. A more global understanding of the portrait makes clear that its performative dimensions go deeper. In the theater of the toilette, Pompadour poses herself at the intersection of gender, class, and emergent racial identities. Each facet of her persona implies its own narrative, from female empowerment to colonial exploitation. But these stories are not mutually exclusive. In painting herself pink, Pompadour demonstrated that she could ably perform more roles than one.

Oliver Wunsch is assistant professor of art history at Boston College; he served as the Maher Curatorial Fellow of American Art at the Harvard Art Museums in 2018–19.